Karma

Freedom and Responsibility

by

Aparna Chakraborty

1998

Kaveri Books

New Delhi–110002

ISBN 81-7479-018-7

Published by : Rakesh Goel

Kaveri Books

4697/5-21A, Ansari Road,

New Delhi- 110002 (India).

Tel : 3288140 Fax : (011) 7198902

Laser Typesetting by : Delite Printers, Delhi.

PRINTED IN INDIA

Dedicated

To

My Mother

Srimati Kadambini Chakraborty

Contents

Foreword

The book is the result of an intensive and critical study on the Indian concepts of *Karma*, Freedom and Responsibility. Law of *karma* is related to freedom which is again related to responsibility, which has been beautifully highlighted by Dr. Aparna Chakraborty. It is not very easy task to cover all the Philosophical systems regarding theories of *karma* etc. This has been successfully accomplished by the scholar, which presupposes her Herculean labour and sincerity to the work.

In the introductory chapter, Dr. Chakraborty has given a brief but substantial account of the law of *karma* accepted in different systems of Indian philosophy like Buddhism, Jainism etc. and their different metaphysical presuppositions in formulating these views, such as the doctrines of impermanence etc. in Buddhism, the existence of subtle matter infra-atomic in size in Jainism etc. Apart from this, the authoress has dealt at length the basic issues concerning law of *karma,* e.g. *jñāna karma- samuccaya- vāda, niṣkāma-karma, sañcita-karma sañciyamāna-karma, prārabdha karma* etc. While discussing the traditional views she has also considered the views of the contemporary thinkers like Dr. Radhakrishnan, Professor Dayakrishna, Dr. Rajendra Prasad etc.

The second chapter deals with *karma* and causation which gives an account of different meaning of the term *'karma'*. Many critical problems like the concept of *kartā*, the relation between *kartā* and *karma* etc. have been raised. She ultimately has come to the conclusion that *karma* cannot be said to be the basic cause of the unity of self and body advocated by different schools of Indian philosophy. She has given sufficient reasons for not accepting the doctrine of *karma* as advocated by the Buddhists, Sāṁkhya philosophers, Nyāya-Vaiśeṣika philosophers, Prābhākaras etc. The authoress has accepted only the Vedānta and Jaina view of *kartā* as satisfactory, which is supported by some arguments.

In the third chapter the scholar has shown a relation between *karma* and *karma phala* and also pointed out some philosophical problems arising out of some factors like difference between *karma* and event, relation between intention and action, relation between the notions of *kartṛtva* and *bhoktṛtva* etc. No *karma phala* theory is to be taken consistent according to her.

In the fourth chapter the scholar has shown the relation between *karma,* freedom and responsibility. To her the denial of freedom contradicts responsibility. The notion of responsibility again is connected with the notion of action. The notion of positive and negative freedom as accepted in the west and the east has been highlighted. To her freedom does not entail arbitrariness. She has beautifully reflected on the views on various concepts of freedom and substantiated Indian standpoint. Dr. Chakraborty has established with the help of logic that the Indian concept of freedom is not incompatible with responsibility and the doctrine of *karma* at least in the context of *jivanmukti.*

The chapter on *karma* and transmigration is also very much interesting on account of the fact that it deals with the relation between *karma* and transmigration. The derivative meaning of the term *'saṁsāra'* is worth-pondering. A few objections have been raised by the scholar and their probable solutions have been suggested.

The chapter six also considers a very important related issue divine intervention which is connected with law of *karma.* It represents a total picture of all the systems of Indian philosophy apart from the *Gītā, Upaniṣad* etc. relating to divine intervention. She has considered at length the critical questions as follows : If God is the controller of everything, He is also the controller of human activities and hence human activities are not under their power and control etc. In this way, it has been shown that the theistic version of the doctrine of *karma* suffers from a lot of philosophical difficulties.

The concluding part of the book contains the major findings like (a) the *karma* presupposes a *kartā,* as the relation between them is based on 'causal structural meaning', (b) the thesis that *karmavādins* do not maintain any logical distinction between the notion of event and action, (c) the relation of *kartā, karma* and *karmaphala* is a causal relation, and (d) self-centric doctrine of *karma* is a consistent one, but the believers in this do not hold it consistently.

The work is the result of Chakraborty's original and analytic thinking . She has shown her excellence in dealing philosophical problems logically. Most of the problems treated here are novel and original in character. She has developed a few arguments in favour of her standpoint, the arguments, I think, are very cogent, interesting and convincing. She deserves congratulations for offering such a work full of logical analysis and originality.

Regarding the theories of *karma* and freedom there is a lot of controversies among the scholars belonging to different systems of Indian philosophy and also among the modern thinkers. The treatment of these theories as done by Dr. Chakraborty is really an 'addition ' to this field, which, I believe, will be appreciated by the scholars in the field. As it does not represent what is said in the tradition, it has got some philosophic charm and flavour which may be liked by the modern scholars.

Dr. Raghunath Ghosh

Department of Philosophy,
University of North Bengal,
West Bengal.

Acknowledgement

It gives me great pleasure to acknowledge my indebtedness to my revered teacher Dr. Jagat Pal under whose supervision and guidance this work has been pursued and completed. I would like to express my heartfelt gratitude to Dr. C. R. Agera, Dr. S.C. Daniel, Dr. N. Malla and Dr. M. Agarwal for taking a keen interest in my work and for making helpful suggestions whenever needed. I am also deeply indebted to Dr. R. Ghosh for his good advice and for his kind foreword to this book. I owe special thanks to the publisher the Kaveri Books, who took a keen interest in publishing this book. Lastly I express my deep sense of gratitude to those writers and authors whose writings directly and indirectly helped me in completion of this book.

Aparna Chakraborty

1

Introduction

The doctrine of *karma* is considered to be one of the most important and fundamental doctrines of classical Indian philosophy. All classical Indian schools of thought except Cārvāka believe in the doctrine of *karma* unquestionably. It is held invariably in the religious, ethical, cultural and philosophical thoughts of the Hindus, the Jainas and the Bauddhas. They all use this doctrine in order to explain and justify different occurrences or happenings found in both anthropocentric and non-anthropocentric worlds. According to them, the root cause of bondage is *karma* and ignorance. Sufferings do not come to us without the antecedent conditions. But when we go into the historical accounts of the doctrine of *karma*, we find that the version of the doctrine of *karma* differs from system to system in both the orthodox and heterodox classical Indian schools of thought. Not only this, even Indological scholars — Indian as well as Western — do not seem to hold the same line of interpretation of the doctrine of *karma*. Their analysis and characterisation of the doctrine of *karma* differ from one another.

Buddhism, for example, believes by and large in the doctrines of impermanency (*anityatā*),[1] momentariness (*kṣaṇabhaṅgavāda*)[2] and non-soul (*anātmavāda*).[3] According to the Buddhists, everything in anthropocentric as well as non-anthropocentric world is necessarily and exceptionally impermanent and subject to production, destruction and change, no matter whether it is a thing or organism or agent or action or result of action. They do not believe in the existence of any permanent being or not-being. For them, everything in the universe is conditional, dependent and relative, and hence is subject to birth and death. The Buddhists do not hold the view that *karma* is governed by a moral administrator of the world i.e., God. According to them, God does not evaluate the moral worth of our actions. He does not decide what we deserve or do not deserve on the account of our deeds. He does not award reward and punishment to us in the forms of happiness and pain. In fact, the Buddhists deny outright the existence of a divine God. For them, *karma* is possible without the involvement of any permanent conscious agency, i.e., *ātmā. Karma* works by itself. The law of *karma* is an impersonal law in the sense that it does not stand in the need of any external agency for its function. It governs the relation of action and its result without the involvement of any mediator. In their view, the *karmic* process is an autonomous process. It does not depend upon any metaphysical entity, self or God. The Buddhists believe in the transmigration of *saṁskāras* (disposition on impressions). But they do not believe in the transmigration of soul. On their account, transmigration of *saṁskāras* is possible without transmigration of a soul from birth to birth. For them, soul is nothing but a bundle of the five fittings or *skandhas, rūpa* or matter, *vedanā* or feeling, *saṁjñā* or perception, *saṁskāra* or disposition and *vijñāna* or consciousness. Buddhism does not believe in the identity of *kartā* (doer) and *bhoktā* (experiencer). Unlike Jainism and Hinduism, Buddhism is of the view that a man may not get the fruit of his *karma* because he is perishable. He may perish before the emergence of the result of his action. Even if he does not perish it is said that he may not realize the fruit of his *karma,* because the fruit of his *karma,* that is *karma phala* is perishable before its doer coming to enjoy or suffer. Not only this, it is also claimed that an individual may be led to some result which is not the result of any of his action. It is because of this reason in Buddhism allocation of responsibility cannot be settled mechanically, as it is possible in Jainism and Hinduism. In Buddhism, it is *karma* which is the root cause of bondage, and liberation is possible only through true knowledge. In the *Dhammapada* it is said that *karma* is birth, *karma* is death, *karma* is pleasure and *karma* is pain. So long as *karma* operates no one can claim to be free from all these afflictions.[4] Since all *karma* is bondage, it has to be got rid of. The moment true knowledge arises all *karmas* are abandoned, uprooted and pulled out of the ground like a palmyra tree and become non-existent and not liable to spring up again in future.[5]

Jainism, like Buddhism, believes that *karma* does not depend on any moral administrator of the world., i.e. God. It is an impersonal law which works by itself without needing any divine agency. Both these systems do not trace the origin of *karma* in the *Vedas* as Hinduism does. They rather criticize and condemn the *Vedic* systems. According to these systems, *karma phala* automatically follows from *karma* without the involvement of any mediator. But, unlike Buddhism, Jainism believes that the doer of action i.e., self or jīva is permanent and beyond production and destruction in its essence. *Karma phala* does not perish before its doer coming to experience it. The doer of action gets the result of his action sooner or later. A man gets what he does and what he gets, it is said, that he deserves it. The Jainas hold that man is wholly responsible for his birth, death and suffering. Whatever he gets is determined by his past deeds. The doer of good gets good result and the doer of bad gets bad result. The Jain's conception of *karma* is different from that of Bauddha's one. According to the Jaina's, *karma* is a subtle matter[6] which is infra-atomic in size and imperceptible, which pulls down the soul (*jīva*) from its spiritual height. The Bauddhas and the Hindus do not believe in the Jaina's materialistic conception of *karma*. According to them, *karma* is not a subtle matter which can be said to be infra-atomic in size. They conceive *karma* as something non-material and formless. But in Jainism both *karma* and *karma phala* are given a material connotation. The Jaina thinkers are of the view that what we suffer or enjoy in the name of *karma phala* is something material pain and material pleasure. Although *karma* in Jainism is considered to be material in nature, but it is said to have a tendency to determine psychic characteristics and produce merit and demerit. For them, *karma* is a special kind of matter-particle which is not metaphysical but real. It enters into the soul or sticks to the soul like oil and dust which stick to clothes and binds it with body. Passions— anger (*krodha),* greed (*lobha),* pride (*māna),* and delusion (*māyā),* are called *kaṣāya* or sticky substances which attract the flow of *karmic* matter into the soul. Passions occur due to ignorance. It is the real cause of bondage. In this respect Jainism agrees with Buddhism, Sāṁkhya and Vedānta. The ideal bondage (*bhāva-bandha*) of the soul takes place as soon as it has bad disposition, and the material bondage (*dravya-bandha*), takes place when there is actual influx of *karma* into the soul. *Karma* particles penetrate into the soul and get accumulated in it according to good and bad deeds. The soul in its intrinsic nature, the Jaina believes, possesses Infinite faith (*ananta-darśana*), Infinite knowledge (*ananta-jñāna*), Infinite bliss (*ananta- sukha*), and Infinite power (*ananta-vīrya*). On their account, all the souls from the lowest to the highest possess consciousness, but the degrees of their consciousness vary according to the obstacles of *karma*. Jainism, like Buddhism, does not admit action without agency and transmigration of *saṁskāras* without transmigrating soul. According to Jaina system, no action is possible without agent i.e., jīva. All actions involve in them a conscious agency which makes them possible. *Saṁskāras* do not transmigrate from birth to birth without a transmigrating soul. They are of the opinion that the soul in its original nature is immaterial and free, but due to *karma* and ignorance it gets united with the body and loses its purity and perfection. Although in Jainism *mukti* is possible through the destruction or exhaustion of the *karmic* matter from the soul, yet the soul's dissociation from *karma* is never thought of as an impossibility. The soul can be dissociated, on their account, from *karma* and body through right knowledge (*samyaka jñāna*), right faith (*samyaka darśana)* and right conduct (*samyaka caritra*). When the soul gets exhausted from the particles of *karma* through right knowledge and action, it is said that the soul shines in its intrinsic nature of infinite knowledge, bliss and power. It transcends *saṁsāra* and goes straight to *siddha-shilā* at the top of the world and dwells there.

Like Jainism and Buddhism, Hinduism also believes in the law of *karma* but its version differs from system to system. For example, Sāṁkhya believes in non-identity of *kartā* and *bhoktā*. In this respect we can say that Sāṁkhya agrees with Buddhism but differs from the other schools of Hinduism i.e., Nyāya, Vaiśeṣika, Mīmāṁsā and Vedānta. Unlike Nyāya-Vaiśeṣika, Mīmāṁsā, Vedānta and Jainism, Sāṁkhya holds that *prakṛti*, an unconscious being, performs action but does not reap the fruit of her action. The fruit of her action is realised by *puruṣa*, a conscious being (self) who does not, and cannot perform actions given its own nature. According to Sāṁkhya, *karma*, no matter whether it is good or bad or indifferent, is the function of *guṇas* of *prakṛti*. It always leads to bondage and not to liberation. Good actions lead to heaven and bad actions to hell. But heaven and hell are subject to bondage. Liberation is possible through knowledge and knowledge alone, and not by *karma*, no matter whether it is performed in a detached or attached manner.

In this respect Sāṁkhya agrees with Advaita Vedānta. Unlike Sāṁkhya, Yoga admits the existence of God and conceives Him to be free from pains, actions, effects and impressions. According to Yoga, God is above the law of *karma.* He is not governed by it. But God does not maintain a moral order of the universe. He does not reward or punish according to merit and demerit of our actions. In this respect Yoga agrees with Buddhism, Jainism and Sāṁkhya but differs from Nyāya-Vaiśeṣika. Unlike them, Nyāya-Vaiśeṣika believes in the existence of God. They are of the opinion that God is a moral administrator of the world. The law of *karma* depends on God for its function. It cannot work by itself, being non-intelligent. God maintains the record of our actions, and awards rewards and punishments according to merit and demerit of our actions. Merit and demerit accrue from our actions. The stock of merit and demerit is called *adṛṣṭa,* the unseen power, which needs the guidance of divine God.

Mīmāṁsā, like Nyāya-Vaiśeṣika, believes in the doctrine of *karma* an unseen power (*apūrva*). According to Mīmāṁsakas, performed actions produce unseen potency (*apūrva*) in the soul of the agent which yields fruit when obstructions are removed and time becomes ripe for its fructification. But, like Nyāya-Vaiśeṣika, Mīmāṁsā does not believe in the existence of God as a mediator between act and its result. The Mīmāṁsakas are of the view that *karma phala* automatically follows from *karma. Karma* has a causal potency (*śakti)* to produce its *karma phala* without the involvement of a divine agency i.e., God. In this respect Mīmāṁsā agrees with Jainism, Buddhism and Sāṁkhya-Yoga. According to this system, through the association of body the soul becomes an agent and enjoyer and this takes place due to *karma.* Like the other systems of thought Mīmāṁsā also believes that the root cause of our bondage is *karma* and ignorance. Unless the obstacles of *karma* are removed the soul cannot be dissociated from the body, the senses and the mind: It cannot shine in its true nature. Prabhākara and Kumāril both admit that abstention from *karma* does not imply abstention from all *karmas,* but abstention from the optional (*vikalpa*) and the prohibited (*niṣiddha*) *karmas* only. Optional actions lead to merit and demerit, but the performance of prohibited actions lead to sin and hell. Kumāril believes in the doctrine of *jñāna-karma samuchchayavāda*. According to him, liberation is possible through knowledge and action, while Prabhākara emphasises on the supremacy of action—though he does not deny knowledge as means of liberation. Advaita Vedānta, like Sāṁkhya, asserts that *mokṣa* is not possible through *karma.* It is possible only through knowledge and knowledge alone. *Karma* helps in purifying our mind, but does not lead to liberation. Without *karma, mokṣa* is possible but without knowledge *mokṣa* is not possible. Rāmānuja, the propounder of *Viśiṣṭādvaita,* like the other Hindu systems of thought, believes that the soul gets united with the body due to ignorance and *karma.* According to him, too, to get liberation the soul has to remove its *karma*-obstacles, and that can be done through a harmonious combination of action and knowledge (*jñāna-karma samuchchaya*). But, unlike the other Hindu systems of thought, he maintains that liberation ultimately comes to us only by the grace of God (*prasāda*). Without God's grace no liberation is possible, even if we perform our actions in a non-attached manner. Rāmānuja, like Nyāya-Vaiśeṣika, holds God as the mediator between action and its result. Unlike Vaiśeṣika, but like latter Naiyāyikas, he believes in the grace of God as means of liberation. All the Hindu systems of thought, except Sāṁkhya, believe, — like Jainism but unlike Buddhism, — in the permanent agency of self. According to them, all actions involve in them a conscious agency. Without conscious agency no action is possible. They believe in the identity of *kartā* and *bhoktā.* They are of the opinion that the doer of action gets the result of his action. *Karma phala* does not perish before its doer coming to realize it. *Ātmā* passes through chain of lives in order to suffer or enjoy the result of action done by it. Unlike Buddhism, Hinduism believes in the deterministic account of the doctrine of *karma.* According to them, the doer of action in its essence is permanent and imperishable. He gets the result of whatever he does in certain form, either in the present life or in the future life. *Karma phala* does not perish without its fructification.

In spite of their sharp differences of opinion and interpretation, all classical Indian systems of thoughts except Cārvāka share this view by and large that whatever is done by the individual leaves behind it some sort of potency which has power to produce happiness and pain either in the present life or in the future life. The law of *kamra* operates in the entire domain of universe—human and non-human— in an inviolable manner and causes bondage. They consider, by and large, knowledge and non-attached action (*niṣkāma-karma*) as necessary conditions to obtain freedom from the obstacles of *karma* and body. They are of the opinion that the acquisition of right knowledge makes the *sancita* (actions which are done in the previous life but have not begun to fructify), and non-attached *sancıyamāna* (actions which are done in the present life) action ineffective by destroying their causal efficacy and enables the agent to obtain freedom from bondage. When the *prārabdha* (actions which have been done in the previous life and have started yielding their fruits) *karmas* exhaust their work, the individual who acts with right knowledge and non-attachment exhausts all his liabilities to rebirth and becomes free. No new *karma* gets accumulated as all *karmas* lose causal energy, and self gets dissociated automatically from body after death. Actions done without attachment or desire do not produce results or consequences which can bind the soul in the cycle of birth, death and rebirth. The soul rises above the merit and demerit of action. Non-attached action serves only as means to attain *mokṣa*. It is not treated as an end in itself. The classical Indian schools of thought take non-attached action in purposive sense. They do not treat them as an end in themselves. All of them agree in holding the view that man is the maker of his own destiny. He is what he does, and he does as he is. The past deeds determine present life, and the deeds of present life determine future life. This chain of life goes in a cyclic way. Except Buddhism, Jainism and Hinduism believe that the soul of man in its essence is free, but due to the association of body it goes under various kinds of sufferings. But all classical Indian schools of thought (except Cārvāka) unquestionably believe in transmigration of *saṁskāras* from birth to birth.

This point has been emphasised by almost all scholars of Indian philosophy. In their view, the doctrine of *karma* is a distinguishing characteristic of Indian philosophy, on the basis of which it can be differentiated from Western philosophy. But so far the nature of the doctrine of *karma* is concerned, whether it is a descriptive doctrine or a moral doctrine or both, about it, interpretations of Indological scholars are not very clear. Sometimes it is interpreted as an extension of the law of 'causation to the sphere of human conduct and teaches that, as every event in the physical world is determined by its antecedents, so everything that happens in the moral realm is preordained'.[7] "It signifies not merely that the events of our life are determined by their antecedent causes, but also that there is absolute justice in the rewards and punishments that fall to our lot.'[8] The rewards and punishments are considered to be the consequences of our actions. Sometimes the law of *karma* is interpreted as the law of conservation of moral energy.[9] It is said that the law of *karma* is the law of conservation of moral values, merits and demerits of actions. [10] This law of conservation means that there is no loss of the effect of work done (*kṛtapraṇāśa*) and that there is no happening of events to a person except as the result of his own work (*akṛtābhyāgama*).[11] 'Whatever action is done by an individual leaves behind it some sort of potency, which has the power to ordain for him joy or sorrow in the future, according as it is good or bad'. [12] An action entitles its doer to some pleasure or pain and, the law operates in such a manner that the doer of action gets what he deserves on the account of his deeds. The function of the law of *karma* is :

> " to equip the individual with the body and the environment which his past career entitles him to. Nature and the events of nature, good and bad, which form the common background of the people of an age or a country are just what are deserved by all of them according to their common moral worth".[13]

Every deed that one performs has its effects in the world and forms within the doer *saṁskāra* or *vāsanā* (tendency) which becomes the basis of his future deeds. *Karma* sets forth the relation between one's action as a *jīva* and one's state of being. Sometimes the law of *karma* is understood not merely in terms of a moral causation. It is identified with a universal principle of causality which applies to all existent entities, human and non-human, in an inviolable manner.

Though the law of *karma* is interpreted by the Indologists in both the senses—moral and non-moral— the moral version of the doctrine of *karma* seems to have been given more prominence than non-moral ones. Except Dasgupta, no other scholar mentioned about *Āyurvedic* conception of the doctrine of *karma*. Most of them emphasize on the moral and spiritual version of it. Hiriyanna, for example, claims that the law of *karma* is not a blind mechanical law. It is essentially ethical.[14] For him, the law of *karma* is immutable, but it is not mechanical in character. Immutability, or inviolability of the law, does not make it mechanical. In the language of Sri

Aurobindo, *karma* is not quite the same thing as a material or substantial law of cause and effect, — the antecedent and its mechanical consequence.[15] For him, *karma* is more than a mechanical law of antecedent and consequent. Humphreys writes :

> "the trouble with several interpretations of the *karma* concept has been that the idea has been understood in a more or less mechanical manner, but to do so is to drain it of all its force, for it could only be properly understood from a spiritual point of view"[16]

Whether the doctrine of *karma* is a universal principle of causality which applies to all existent entities, or is a moral law which applies to human beings and human beings alone, is no doubt a matter of philosophical importance. But we have not entered into this debate. We have taken for granted the moral version of the doctrine of *karma,* which is widely held by almost all the Indologists— Indian as well as non-Indian. We have, thus, restricted the use of the doctrine of *karma.* We have considered it only in the domain of human beings and their conduct. The domains of non-human beings fall outside the scope of our discussion.

Many Indologists trace the origin of the doctrine of *karma* in the *Rigvedic* concepts of *Ṛta* and sacrifice. In their view the ideas of *Ṛta* and sacrifice contain in them the germs of the law of *karma.* According to Radhakrishnan, "*Ṛta* is an anticipation of the law of *karma.* "[17] S.N. Dasgupta observes :

> "When the sacrifice is performed, the action leaves an unseen magical virtue, called *adṛṣṭa* (the unseen) or the *apūrva* (new), that by it the desired object will be achieved in a mysterious manner, for the *modus operandi* of the *apūrva* is unknown. There is also the notion prevalent in the *Saṁhitās* .... that he who commits wicked deeds suffers in another world, whereas he who performs good deeds enjoys the highest material pleasures. These were probably associated with the conception of *Ṛta,* the inviolable order of things. Thus these are probably the elements which built up the *karma*

> theory which we find pretty well established but not emphasized in the *Upaniṣads* where it is said that according to good or bad actions men will have good or bad births."[18]

It is said that the *Rigvedic* term *'Ishṭāpūrta'* indicates nothing but the fund of merit and demerit earned by making offerings to God and gifts to the priests. Sacrifice *(yajña)* is taken in the sense of *karma* and consequence of sacrifice is taken in the sense of *phala*. The *Rigvedic* concept *Ṛta* is identified with the doctrine of *karma* in moral sphere. [19] Sometimes it is said that the concept of *karma* was a new addition to Upaniṣadic thought.Western Indologists are of the opinion that the doctrine of *karma* was developed through the social conflict between the *Brahmins* and the *Kshatriyas*. Garbe, for example, holds that in opposition to the *Brahminical* systems the *Kshatriyas* formulated two dominant concepts — the metaphysics of monistic Absolutism and the ethical law of *karman*. The conflict between these two sections expressed itself also at an intellectual level, and the *Kshatriyas* were the spokesmen of more enlightened notions against the traditional theology and conservative dogmatism of the hieratic sections.[20] While some scholars maintain that the concept of *karma* has a composite structure. It has come from both the *Vedic* and non-*Vedic* sources. They are of the view that though the doctrine of *karma* had an Aryan origin, yet the doctrine was not altogether absent from the primitive people. They trace its root in the notions of the primitive tribes regarding the potency of certain magical character of 'sacred actions'.[21] According to Dasgupta,

> "the law of *karman* was thus rooted in the Indian mind from the earliest days in the tribal belief in the efficacy of magical operations, incantations and the like, and it was only extended at a later stage into the ethical field. "[22]

Whether the doctrine of *karma* had its root in the *Rigveda* or was borrowed from non-Aryan sources, or whether it was developed through the social conflict between *Brahmins* and *Kshatriyas* or not, or whether it is an extension of beliefs present in early *Vedic* times or was a new addition to *upaniṣadic*, Jaina, Bauddha's thought or not, no doubt, is a matter of historical importance. But philoso phically it is not important. That is the reason why we have not entered into this debate.

But in spite of the great importance accorded to the law of *karma* by the Indologists— Indian as well as non-Indian — it has not been given a conceptual analysis which is very important from the philosophical point of view to understand the intelligibility of the doctrine of *karma.* Dayakrishna and Rajendra Prasad have attempted to give a conceptual analysis of the doctrine of *karma.* But in the process they have raised a number of conceptual issues which deserve a closer attention on the part of researchers. It is hoped that the study undertaken here is the extension of such a spirit. Unless we analyse the concepts of *karma* and *karma phala* and their relation to *kartā,* we cannot understand the doctrine of *karma* in a fruitful manner. Because these concepts are found invariably involved in the assertions of the doctrine of *karma.* The notion of *karma* is conceptually connected with the notions of *saṁsāra,* transmigration, freedom and responsibility. In order to understand the notion of *karma* a philosophical analysis of the notions of *saṁsāra,* transmigration, freedom and responsibility is also required at which the present book aims. The objective of this book is not to ascertain the truth or falsity, validity or invalidity, of the doctrine of *karma,* nor even to make a historical study of the different versions and interpretations of the doctrine of *karma*. It also does not make any attempt to discover some hitherto unknown truth about it. What it intends to do is its philosophical analysis through the analysis of the notions of *kartā, karma* and *karma phala* and some other related notions like the notions of transmigration, freedom responsibility, *saṁsāra, mokṣa* and divine intervention in order to understand and comprehend its meaningfulness and intelligibility which is philosophically more important. Because investigation into the meaning of the doctrine of *karma* comes logically prior to the considerations of its truth, evidence, validity and legitimacy. If the doctrine of *karma* is an unintelligible doctrine, then the question of its truth or validity cannot legitimately be raised. That is the reason why we have made a humble attempt to enquire into the meaning and the intelligibility of the doctrine of *karma* through its analysis and the analysis of some other related concepts. Via an analytical examination we have tried to show that no classical version of the doctrine of *karma* i.e., Jainism, Buddhism and Hinduism is coherent and satisfactory. A coherent and satisfactory account of the doctrine of *karma* leads us not only to monisticism and self-centric view of *karma* but also makes social, moral and religious inter-personal, interactions impossible which the *karmavādins* themselves would not like to hold from socio-moral religious points of view.

Notes and References

1. J. N. Sinha, *Outlines of Indian Philosophy*, New Central Book Agency, Calcutta, 2nd Edition, 1985, p. 82.
2. C. D. Sharma, *A Critical Survey of Indian Philosophy*, Motilal Banarsidass, p. 74.
3. J. N. Sinha, *op. cit.*, p. 86.
4. *Dhammapada*, p. 335.
5. H. C. Warren, *Buddhism in Translations*, pp. 216-17.
6. J. N. Sinha, *op. cit.*, p. 119.
7. M. Hiriyanna, *The Essentials of Indian Philosophy*, London, George Allen and Unwin, 1949, p. 46.
8. *Ibid.*, p. 48.
9. S. Radhakrishnan, *Indian Philosophy* , Vol. I, London, George Allen & Unwin, p. 245.
10. S. C. Chatterjee & D. M. Datta, *An Introduction to Indian Philosophy*, Calcutta, University of Calcutta, 8th Edition, 1984, p. 15.
11. *Ibid.*, p. 15.
12. S. N. Dasgupta, *A History of Indian Philosophy*, Vol. I, Cambridge, Cambridge University Press, 1922, p. 71.
13. D. M. Datta, *Philosophical Perspectives : A Selection of Essays*, Patna, Bharati Bhawan, 1971, p. 93.
14. Rajendra Prasad, *Karma, Causation and Retributive Morality*, Munshiram Manoharlal Publishers Pvt. Ltd., New Delhi, 1989, P. 220.
15. Sri Aurobindo, *The Problem of Rebirth*, Sri Aurobindo Ashram Press, Pondicherry, 1952, p. 99.
16. Humphreys, *Karma and Rebirth*, p. 12.
17. S. Radhakrishnan, *Indian Philosophy*, Vol. I, p. 109.
18. S. N. Dasgupta, *A History of Indian Philosophy*, Cambridge University Press, Vol. I, 1963, p. 73.
19. Gopalan, *Hindu Social Philosophy*, Wiley Eastern Limited, New Delhi, 1979, p. 25.
20. Vishwanath Prasad Varma, *Early Buddhism and Its Origins.*, Munshiram Manoharlal Publishers Pvt. Ltd., 1973.
21. L. Thorndike, *A History of Magic and Experimental Science*, Vol. II, New York, 1923.
22. S. N. Dasgupta, *Indian Idealism*, p. 3.

2

Karma and Causation

When we reflect upon the notion on *karma* we find that there is no one particular meaning which can be said to be found invariably in all its uses, or with reference to which we can intelligibly talk about it in all sorts of its applications. It is used in different senses in different systems. Mostly the word '*karma*' is taken to indicate 'an action', 'a work' or 'a deed'. It is derived from the root '*kṛ*', which means 'to do', and therefore is defined in the sense of an action, a work or a deed. From this point of view, *karmas* are generally divided into three kinds: mental, vocal and bodily. Thinking, willing, desiring, comparing and imagining are called mental *karmas.* Talking and speaking are called vocal *karmas.* Breathing, hearing and seeing are called bodily *karmas.* Sometimes *karmas* are classified as moral, immoral and non-moral; religious, irreligious and non-religious; *Vedic* and non-*Vedic;* spiritual and non-spiritual; voluntary and non-voluntary; good, evil and neutral etc.

Mīmāṁsā classifies actions into obligatory (which must be performed), optional (which may or may not be performed) and prohibited (which must not be performed). Vaiśeṣika, divides actions into five classes: (i) upward movement (*utkṣepaṇa*), (ii) downward movement (*avakṣepaṇa*), (iii) contraction (*ākuñcana*), (iv) expansion (*prasāraṇa),* and (v) locomotion (*gamana*). Jaina classifies *karmas* as *gotra-karma* (the *karma* that determines the family into which one is born), *āyuṣ karma* (the *karma* that determines the length of life), *jñānāvaraṇiya karma* (the *karma* that clouds knowledge), *darśanāvaraṇiya karma* (the *karma* that clouds faith) *mohanīya karma* (the *karma* that produces delusion), *vedanīya karma* (the *karma* that produces emotions of pleasure and pain). Sāṃkhya divides actions into three classes: (i) *sāttvika,* (ii) *rājasika* and (iii) *tāmasika. Sāttvika* action is that kind of action which produces pleasure in its various forms, such as, satisfaction, joy, happiness, bliss, contentment, etc. *Rājasika* action is that kind of action which is of the nature of pain (*duḥkha*), and which causes all painful experiences in our life. *Tāmasika* action is that kind of action which induces sleep, drowsiness and laziness. *Gītā* divides action into two classes: attached action (*sakāma karma*) and detached action (*niṣkāma karma*). In *Rigveda 'karma'* is used in the sense of sacrificial action (*yajña*).

Sometimes the word *'karma'* is used to refer not only to an action but also the result of action. It is said that the result is a part of the action. They are inseparable although are logically distinguishable. Their relation is invariable relation. The results which they produce are of three-fold. It gives the doer an appropriate reward or punishment. It determines the nature of the doer. Action leaves impression or tendency in the agent which is called *saṁskāra* in the classical Indian systems of thought. Mīmāṁsā calls it *apūrva* (unseen potency). The *apūrva* is conceived as link between action and its fruit. It is a causal potency (*śakti*) in the act which leads to its fructification. Therefore it may be regarded either as the imperceptible antecedent of the fruit, or as the after-state of the act. It is said that the theory of *apūrva* is a limited hypothesis which tries to explain a part of the general problem of conservation of the fruits of all actions—ritualistic and non-ritualistic— which the moral universal law of *karma* seeks to explain.

In Nyāya-Vaiśeṣika, *karma* is regarded as *adṛṣṭa* (unseen power) *Adṛṣṭa* is conceived as the sum total of merits and demerits accruing from our past actions which produces joys and sorrows. But since *adṛṣṭa,* on the Nyāya-Vaiśeṣika account, is an unintelligent principle, it cannot by itself lead to joys and sorrows which arise due to our past actions. So it is argued that *adṛṣṭa* must be guided by some intelligent agent to produce its proper consequences. Individual selves cannot, on their views, direct or control *adṛṣṭa,* for they do not know anything about the *adṛṣṭa.* So the intelligent agent who guides *adṛṣṭa* through the proper channels to produce the proper effects, is the eternal, omnipotent and omniscient divine being. It is God who controls our *adṛṣṭa* and dispenses all joys and sorrows of our life strictly in accordance with it. Therefore God is said to be the giver of the fruits of our deeds (*karmaphalapradātā*). The principle which is called by Mīmāṁsā as *apūrva* and Nyāya-Vaiśeṣika as *adṛṣṭa* is called by Buddhism as *vāsanā*. It is believed that *saṁskāras* function as determinants to agent's future action and nature. Keeping the *phala* of *karma* in view, *karmas* are generally classified into three categories : *sancita* (accumulated impressions), *prārabdha* (fructifying impressions) and *kriyamāna* (current impressions). *Sancita karma* is called the accumulated impressions of the deeds of the past life, which have not yet begun to fructify. *Prārabdha karma* is called the impressions of the past deeds which have already started yielding the fruits. *Kriyamāna karma* is called the impressions of the present deeds which are being accumulated by performing actions in the present life. *Karma* is often taken to indicate a 'law of *karma*' or a 'principle of causality' with special reference to moral action. Sometimes it is loosely designated as a doctrine. Sometimes it refers to universal principle of causality which applies to all existent entities. Sometimes it refers to the joint doctrine of the law of *karma*, —the principle of causality which holds that all moral actions produce moral effects, and of *saṁsāra*—the principle that there is a transmigration of the self (the *sūkṣmaśarīra*) or 'subtle body' in a series of births, deaths and rebirths.[1] *Karma* in the sense of moral law is used in both the senses : descriptive and ethical. In the descriptive sense, it states that good and bad actions done by the doer produce good and bad results respectively, which the doer of actions realizes in the forms of happiness and pain, either in the present life, or in the future life. In the ethical sense, it states that man is responsible for whatever he does and whatever he does, he also deserves it (as he sows so shall he reap). In Jainism, *karma* is used in the sense of material particles which unite the soul to the body. Ignorance of truth and four passions—anger (*krodha*), greed (*lobha*), pride (*māna*) and delusion (māyā) which are called *kaṣāya* or sticky substances where *karmic* particles stick— attract the flow of *karmic* matters towards the soul. The state when *karmic* particles actually begin to flow towards the soul to bind it is called *āsrava* or flow. The state when these particles actually infiltrate into the soul and bind it is called *bandha* or bondage. By the possession and practice of right faith, right knowledge and right conduct, the influx of fresh *karma* is stopped. This state in Jainism is called *samvara* or stoppage. When the existing *karmas* get exhausted that state is called *nirjarā* or wearing out. When the last particle of *karma* gets completely exhausted the partnership between soul and matter is dissolved, and the soul shines in its intrinsic nature of infinite faith, infinite knowledge, infinite bliss and infinite power. This state in Jainism is called *mokṣa* or liberation.

Thus, it is quite obvious from the above discussions that there is no one particular meaning of the word *'karma'* which can be said to be found invariably in all its applications in the different classical Indian systems of thought. Its use differs from system to system. But without pre-judging the issue which system has used the word *'karma* , correctly, we shall use it in the sense of 'action'. The word 'action' is not an unambiguous word. Philosophers have used it in different senses. MacMurray, for example, claims that "to act is to effect a change in the external world .... Action proceeds from the self to the world. It terminates in things, not in ideas".[2] According to this definition of action, unless we bring about change in the external world, what we do cannot be called an action. No doubt, it is true that such effected changes are called actions, but we don't see any reason for restricting the application of action to external changes only, because even without effecting a change in the external world it is possible for us to do something. When we use the term *'karma'* in the sense of action, it includes in its meaning not only those actions whose effects are changes in the external world, but also those whose effects are limited to the inner life of the actor. Sometimes by 'action' is meant only such of our doings which can be the objects of our moral evaluation, and sometimes anything we do without bothering whether or not it can be morally evaluated. But here we are concerned with action in general sense, and therefore, the analysis of the concept of *karma* attempted in this chapter would be an analysis of action in general, no matter whether it is sacrificial action or not; whether it is moral action or not; whether it is attached action or not. That is because whatever *karma* is done, it is claimed by and large that it binds the doer to realise its result in the present life or in the future life, (life after death) sooner or later.

When we analyse the notion of *karma* in the sense of action, we find that it necessarily involves in it a reference to an agent (*kartā*) who causes it. Without *kartā* no *karma* can be conceived to be possible. This is one of the most essential characteristics of the notion of *karma* (action). The notion of *karma* is conceptually connected with the notion of *kriyā* (activity) and the notion of *kriyā* is conceptually connected with the notion of *kartā*. *Karma* without *kriyā* is not possible and *kriyā* without *kartā* is not conceivable. The meaning of one consists in the meaning of other. If it is true that action without activity is not possible and the notion of *kartā* is conceptually connected with the notion of activity, the notion of *kartā* also cannot be understood without making a reference to the notion of *karma*. The *kartā* is not a *kartā* without *karma* and the *karma* is not a *karma* without *kartā*. The meaning of one involves in it a reference to the meaning of the other. No one becomes *kartā* without action. A man becomes *kartā* by doing action. Actions are always done by somebody. Therefore, we cannot say that X is an action nor can we ask the question: Who did it? unless we presuppose the existence of *kartā*. It is quite possible that we may fail to determine the doer of certain action but that does not amount to mean that action is possible without doer. No action is conceivable without doer. Actions are always done by somebody, otherwise they will not be actions at all. In this sense actions are not events. Events happen, whereas actions are done. The theists who regard events as the deeds of God make the class of events null. For them, there is no such thing called as an event. What we call as an event, the theists call that as an action of God. For them, events and actions do not belong to two different logical categories.

Here one might ask this question : Who is *kartā* ? The answer is quite obvious. A *kartā* is one who does or performs actions, or brings about changes in the existing states of affairs. If the question is asked : What is action? The answer again is quite obvious. Action is that which is done and the notion of doing involves in it the notion of change. This implies that no one can be a *kartā* without doing, and to do is to act, hence no one can be a *kartā* without being active. The notion of doing is connected with the notion of action and the notion of action has no meaning apart from and independent of, the notion of doing. The meaning of one involves in it the meaning of other. Doing without action is not possible and action without doing is not conceivable. Therefore one of the essential characteristics for any being to be a *kartā* is that he must be an active being. He must have the efficacious power to do or to act or to bring about certain changes in the existing state of affairs. If he has no efficacious power to bring about action, or action does not originate from him, he cannot be said to be a *kartā*. He ceases to be a *kartā*. In fact, when no action is done, the question of somebody's being a *kartā* simply does not arise at all. The question of somebody's being a *kartā* does arise only when he performs certain actions. A person becomes a *kartā* just by doing action no matter whether what he performs is moral or non-moral. An inactiveness notion of *kartā* is self-contradictory in terms. No action can originate from someone unless it is presupposed that he has a power to originate or to bring about action and that would not be possible unless his existence is presupposed. If somebody does not exist, he cannot originate action nor can he be characterized as a *kartā* . Therefore for somebody to be a *kartā*, he must have substantial existence. In fact, when somebody does not exist, the question of originating of action from him or his being as a *kartā* of certain actions does not simply arise at all. But that does not mean that he cannot conceivably exist unless he does something. A thing can be conceived to be existing even when it does not do anything and that is logically quite possible because the notion of existence is not conceptually connected with the notion of doing. To exist is not to do, but doing is not possible without being existing. As a matter of fact, there are many things in the universe which exist but do not perform any sort of action, i.e., material objects, animals, insects and birds etc. Therefore it would be wrong to say that existence without doing is not conceivable. And to say this, however, does not mean that doing without existence is possible. It is perfectly true that somebody may have an efficacious power to cause action and yet he may not execute his power in bringing about action or refraining from it. But simply on that ground he cannot be regarded as a *kartā* because no one becomes a *kartā* on the basis of his efficacious power unless he executes that power in bringing about the action. Having power is one thing and executing of that power is another thing, and both the notions are logically unconnected because somebody may be conceived to have potential power and yet he may not execute that power. Actions occur when power is executed and the execution of power either in bringing about action or refraining from it always requires some conscious efforts on the part of the agent. And no one can be said to be making some conscious efforts unless he exhibits them in action. From this point of view, action can be said to be a criterion to judge whether someone is really making conscious efforts or not. Actions are done and doing is not possible without assuming the existence of a conscious being. Therefore the doer of action cannot be any unconscious being. Only conscious beings can be said to be the doer of actions because they are the only beings who have powers not only to do certain actions but also to refrain from doing them at their free wills. Conscious beings are conceived to have powers of choosing, deciding, planning, intending, aiming and thinking etc. with which our notion of action is essentially connected. In doing of action the doer not only experiences that he is acting but also feels that it is his action, and he is doing it because of this reason he thinks that he is responsible for whatever he does and whatever he does, he also deserves its fruit. This is what the doctrine of *karma* states. It asserts that to do an action is to be responsible for its result, good or bad. If that be so, animals, insects and birds etc. fall outside the domain of our conception of action. Only in the context of human beings the concept of action has its legitimate applicability.

All actions are caused and whatever is caused is an event. From this point of view, we can say that actions are also a kind of events and come under the realm of the causation theory. But that does not mean that whatever is caused is an action. Whatever is caused may or may not be an action because to cause is not to do. To cause is to originate or to produce or to bring something about, which is quite different from that of doing. Something may cause something else, and yet what causes that may not be a *kartā*, and what is caused may not be an action. This is perfectly quite conceivable. All instances of causation are not the instances of doing, though all instances of doing are the instances of causation. Since to cause is not to do; therefore something may cause something else without doing of it. But doing of something is not possible without causing of it. Because to do is to cause. This means that the notion of doing involves in it the notion of causation but the notion of causation does not involve in it the notion of doing. For example, fire has a causal power to produce smoke but fire, on that ground, cannot be said to be a *kartā* of smoke, nor can the production of smoke be said to be an action of fire. Fire has only a causal or an efficacious power to produce smoke but it has no agential power. Fire cannot refrain itself from producing smoke if dry leaves are put on it. But a *kartā* has power not only to cause certain actions by his will but also to refrain himself from causing certain actions which fire does not have. Fire cannot be said to be doing things against its will because it has no will. While in the case of a *kartā* we can very well say that he can do certain things against his will because he has will. As a matter of fact, there are many cases where individuals perform actions against their will, which are generally classified under the category of compelled actions. A *kartā* has will power to make or not to make certain changes in the existing state of affairs. Due to will power a *kartā* can change his course of actions, if he decides, which fire cannot do. Fire has no decisive power to change its course of events. Further more, a *kartā* has power to choose or not to choose different courses of action. He has power not only to cause an action but also not to cause it. A *kartā* can control his actions if he decides, which fire cannot do. The relation that holds between *kartā* and his *karma* is not purely a causal and mechanical relation in the sense that under certain antecedent conditions a *kartā* is bound to produce certain actions. But the relation that holds between fire and smoke is a causal and mechanical relation. Fire produces smoke when certain antecedent conditions are present. Fire and smoke relation can be understood purely in deterministic terms but *kartā* and *karma* relation cannot be understood in deterministic terms nor can it be characterized purely as mechanical in nature. Due to the involvement of the elements of cognition, volition, desire and passion, actions cannot be said to have predictability like natural events. What course of action a *kartā* would be doing cannot be predicted accurately in advance, no matter how much knowledge one may have about the antecedent conditions of a *kartā*. But in the cases of natural events accurate predictability is quite possible,—provided we have sufficient knowledge about the events. An event may have a causal power of producing but it has no power of refraining. It cannot refrain itself from causing something when certain antecedent conditions are present. It is because of this reason the will power of a *kartā* cannot be said to be identical with the power of a cause. Will has power of causing, but a cause has no power of willing. Because of this reason certain words which make sense in the context of *kartā* do not make any sense in the context of fire or events. For example, the words 'compel', 'responsibility', 'accountability, 'deservability' and 'experiencing of reward and punishment' in the forms of pleasure and pain do not have any meaning in the context of fire and events but they do have meanings in the context of *kartā* and his actions. The reason why such words do have meaningful applicability in the cases of *kartā* and actions is that a *kartā* can exert his will power over other things, and thus can change their courses of action which fire and event cannot do because they lack will power. Fire can produce smoke when certain antecedent conditions are present but it cannot control and change the events of smoke. Above all, actions are conscious phenomena. They always involve in them a reference to some conscious agency who is believed to have powers of cognizing, experiencing, feeling, willing, and desiring etc. which fire and events lack. Actions being conscious phenomena cannot be said to have their origins from unconscious things like fire and events. Material things and events, thus, cannot legitimately be characterized as *kartā* even if they have powers of causing certain events nor can what they cause be said to be actions. The role of a *kartā* is not just to cause action, but also to do a lot of other things, which are required by actions before causing them i.e., deliberation, planning, choosing, etc. which material objects and events cannot do. Therefore they fall outside the domain of the universe of actions.

If the above view is correct, it is quite obvious that the notions of *kartā* and *karma* are different from the notions of causes and events respectively. (By events we mean those kinds of happenings which do not involve in them the notion of agency i.e., conscious being). All cases of action can be said to be the cases of events since they are caused by a *kartā* , but all cases of events cannot be said to be the cases of action, since most of them do not originate from any agency i.e., natural events. Which means that the notion of event does not essentially involve in it the notion of agency. Events cannot be characterized as agential in nature. They can be conceived apart from and independent of a conscious agency, human or divine. Events occur when certain antecedent conditions are present without the role of any conscious being working as agency behind them. Since events do not conceptually involve in them the notion of agency, they cannot be said to be the cases of action. 'Doing' has no meaning in the context of events. Events just happen depending upon their antecedent conditions. One event may cause another event, but what is caused cannot be said to be the result of some conscious agency. While, on the contrary, actions are always done. Since they are always done; therefore it makes no sense to say that there are certain cases which are the cases of action, but are not caused by anybody. Actions are conscious phenomena in the sense that they are always brought about through conscious efforts and activities. They just do not occur like events when certain antecedent conditions are present. Actions occur when conscious efforts are made, and agential power is executed, which is not possible without the admissibility of the existence of a conscious being. Conscious efforts always require a conscious being. That is because it is the conscious being who makes a conscious effort to bring about actions by exerting and executing his power which can neither be done by events, mental or physical, nor by material objects i.e., body. Body and bodily events do not have power to play the role of a conscious agency which the notion of action essentially involves in it. But saying this does not mean that body and bodily movements are in no way connected with the notion of action. Body and bodily movements no doubt are causally connected with action. But on that ground they cannot be said to be the *kartā* of action. Actions originate from the agent and his beliefs, intentions, desires, wills and body. Conscious being and his roles are one of the essential conditions for any action to happen, which are not required by events to happen. That is because events are not conceptually connected with any conscious agency as actions are connected. Moreover, actions are purposive in character; they are consciously willed, planned and pursued unlike events. But this, however, does not mean that actions are uncaused. Actions are not uncaused. All actions are caused. But to say that they are caused is not to say that they are purposive in character. If it were so, all events would be purposive in character since they are caused. But this is not true. Actions do not become purposive on the ground of their being caused. Actions become purposive when they are consciously willed to attain certain goals, — worldly or non-worldly. Events are mechanical in character in the sense that they just happen when certain other events are present. They are not brought about through conscious efforts and activities as actions are done. Events are neither intended nor aimed, whereas actions are intended and aimed. The purposive character of actions, thus, rules out the logical possibility of events or material things as the sources of their origin. No events, whether they are mental or physical, do have any power to fulfil the logical requirements of action which an action requires for its origination. Conscious beings and that too human beings are the only beings who can be said to have powers to satisfy the logical requirements of action, and such beings can neither be analysed merely in terms of psycho-physical elements or events, nor can their roles be determined causally and mechanically. That is the reason why only conscious beings can legitimately be characterized as *kartā* of *karma*. It is the characteristic of *karma* (action) that it is either obeyed or disobeyed or left undone. It may or may not be performed unlike event. So for anything to be a *kartā*, that thing must have power not only to obey or discbey actions, but also to refrain from doing them, which no material objects including bodily events do have, except conscious beings, even if they are causally connected. Conscious beings are the only beings who can be said to have powers not only to do an action, but also to refrain from doing it, as and when they want. Body and bodily movements, no doubt, do play causal roles in the origination of action. Action without body and bodily muscle contractions cannot be conceived to happen. From this point of view, we can say that the notion of action not only involves a reference to an agent i.e., conscious being, but also to the body and bodily movements. Agent's beliefs, attitudes, cognitions, desires, passions, intentions and motives may play causal roles in certain sense in the origination of actions. But none of these elements can be assigned with the role of *kartā* since they lack agential characteristics which an action essentially requires to happen. For any agent to do an action he must have a body. But his body cannot by itself initiate action, in spite of its being causally related, unless the agent himself, that is, a conscious being initiates it. Action occurs when the agent executes his powers, and powers cannot be executed without assuming the existence of the agent. So we can say that no action can be made possible without the involvement of a conscious agency. Agent and his beliefs, intentions and bodily muscle contractions together can play, and in fact they do play, causal roles in the origination of actions. It is perfectly quite possible because they are quite compatible. When we say that actions are conscious phenomena because they are produced through conscious activities and efforts, that should not be taken to mean that actions cannot be done in ignorance and under compulsions. Actions can be done in ignorance and under compulsions because conscious activities and efforts can be made in ignorance and under compulsions. To perform conscious activities and make conscious efforts is not always to do right actions. It is quite possible that an agent may go wrong in his choosing and planning of certain actions. But that would not amount to mean that he does not perform conscious activities and make conscious efforts. As a matter of fact, most of us perform conscious activities and make conscious efforts not only in ignorance but also under certain internal and external constraints.

If, we admit for the sake of argument that the notion of action does not essentially involve in it a reference to the notion of a conscious agency and is interpretable in terms of events alone, then what the doctrine of *karma* asserts becomes meaningless. It makes no sense to say that the doer of action gets the result of his action and he deserves the result of what he does. The doer of good gets good result and the doer of bad gets bad result and no doer gets reverse result of his action. The *karmic* assertions make sense only when we assume that the notion of *karma* (action) essentially involves in it a reference to some conscious agency who not only causes action, but also reaps the result of his action. They do not make any sense, if the notion of action is interpreted merely in terms of events without assuming some conscious agent behind the occurrences of events. In other words, the doctrine of *karma* and its assertions do have meanings only in the agent-cause paradigm of action, — the paradigm in which action originates from an agent. They do not have any meaning in the non-agent-cause paradigm of action, that is, event-cause paradigm of action,—the paradigm in which an event rather than an agent is conceived as a source of action. In fact, in the event-cause paradigm of action no distinction between *kartā* and cause, action and event is maintained. Both the notions of *kartā* and 'action' are interpreted solely in terms of events, and events alone, wherein, *karmic* assertions do not have any meaning because what they assert fall outside the domain of the event—cause paradigm of action. Events cannot be held to be morally responsible and accountable nor can they be said that they realize good and bad consequences of their actions, because they do not perform action in the context of which the notions of moral responsibility and accountability do have meanings. Such words do have meanings only in the agent-cause paradigm of action. They do not have meaningful applicability in the event-cause paradigm of action. In fact, in the context of event-cause paradigm of action the question of event's being responsible and accountable does not arise at all. But saying all these, however, do not amount to mean that an agent can do actions without involving his body and bodily movements. No agent can do any action without his body and bodily movements because body and bodily movements are essential components of action. But to say this does not mean that body and bodily movements perform actions. Body and bodily movements do not, and cannot, perform actions by themselves unless agent executes his power. Psycho-physical events no doubt are causally involved in the production of actions, but none of these events can legitimately be characterized as *kartā* since they do not, and cannot, play the agential role of *kartā* which actions require to happen. The notion of action essentially involves in it the notion of *kartā* which makes action possible. No action is conceivable apart from, and independent of, a conscious agency. The notion of *kartā* is neither reducible to body nor is it analysable in terms of its bodily movements.

There is no doubt that one action may generate another action, but action which comes first in order of the series of actions does not originate from any other action. It originates from the agent, directly through the involvement of bodily efforts. Such actions may be characterized as basic or primitive actions since they originate directly from the agent and come first in the order of the series of actions. But actions which get generated by some other actions cannot be said to be the basic actions. They are non-primitive actions. Sometimes actions are divided into basic and non-basic classes keeping their ends in view. It is said that actions which are aimed or desired are basic actions and actions which are used as means to attain them are non-basic actions. But the latter sense is different from the former one. When we use the word 'basic action', we use it in the former sense, not in the latter sense of the term. Basic actions are direct actions which come first in the order of the series of actions connected and are brought about by the agent through his bodily efforts. This view of action goes against the event-causalist's account. Because in the event-causality account, actions can be interpreted and explained solely in terms of certain events like intending, wanting, believing, without making any reference to a metaphysical entity called agent who not only intends, wants, believes, deliberates and chooses but also sets the process of action. For them, intentions and beliefs etc. alone cause a man to commit an action which in our account of action is not possible. Because, according to our account, no action can happen without involving a reference to some conscious agent, who himself carries out intentions and beliefs etc. which are quite often causally associated with actions. No agent can cause any action, if he himself remains inactive. In fact, he cannot be called as an agent at all. Somebody becomes an agent only when he performs action. If he does not perform any action and remains inactive, he cannot be said to be an agent at all. The question of his being an agent simply does not arise. Although bodily movements are undoubtedly essential components of action but they are not actions themselves. Just as sight without eye is not possible but eye is not sight. Likewise, no action without bodily movements is possible. But bodily movements themselves are not actions. Neither mental nor bodily events by themselves are capable of giving sufficient explanation of action. If mental and bodily events were the basic sources of action, and not the agent, it would have been possible to explain the notion of action solely in terms of them. But since it is not possible to explain the notion of action (i.e., intentional action) in terms of certain psycho-physical events without making a reference to an agent who initiates the events. The psycho-physical events cannot be said to be the basic resources of action. In fact, the distinction between mental and physical events cannot be maintained without assuming a conscious metaphysical entity i.e., self.

From the foregoing discussions thus, it is quite obvious that *karma* cannot be said to be the basic cause of the unity of self and body which is generally advocated by different classical Indian systems of thought because the notion of the unity of self and body logically precedes the notion of *karma.* It is the unity of self and body which makes basic *karma* possible and what makes it possible cannot be explained by referring to it, as the classical Indian thinkers advocated; nor can it be said to be the cause of the beginning of birth or individual existence as the *karmavadins* believe.

Actions are classified in different ways : voluntary and involuntary, conditional and unconditional, occasional and non-occasional, attached and detached, good and bad, pleasurable and painful, compelled and uncompelled, obligatory, prohibitory and optional etc. Whatever action may be it essentially involves in it the notion of agency, in the sense that it is always caused by an agent. Agent is the controller and the authority of all actions. The sources or the grounds from which actions ultimately originate is the agent (*kartā*) himself. If the notion of agency is dissociated from the notion of action, an action cannot be differentiated from an event. Because it is the notion of *kartā* involved in the notion of *karma* which differentiates *karma* from event. All occurrences of phenomena can broadly be divided into two categories : agent-caused phenomena (i.e., action events or simply actions) and non-agent caused phenomena (i.e., non-action events or simply events.) All actions are events since they are caused by the agent, but all events are not actions since most of them are not caused by the agent. Therefore to identify *karma* with event would amount to committing a logical mistake. Action (*karma*) is logically and conceptually grounded in the notion of *kartā*. Without the association of the notion of *kartā* (agent), no event can be regarded as an action.

From our analysis it becomes quite obvious that the Buddhists doctrine of *karma* cannot be said to be consistent and intelligible. Because Buddhism denies the existence of a permanent self. They believe in a temporary self and reduce the self to psycho-physical organism, and treat it as a bundle of the five *skandhas* — *rūpa* (matter), *vedanā* (feeling), *saṁjñā* (perception), *saṁskāra* (disposition) and *vijñāna* (consciousness). And these *skandhas* cannot play, given their nature, separately or jointly the agential role, that is, the role of a substantial conscious being. *Karma* always presupposes the existence of *kartā*, a substantial conscious being. The Buddhists account of self does not fulfil this logical requirement of the doctrine of *karma.* It fails to satisfy the conditions of a *kartā*. The Buddhists' self has not agential power which an action requires for its origination. Buddhism does not in fact maintain any distinction between *kartā* and cause, action and event. It rather advocates the view that action without a substantial conscious agent is possible which our conception of *karma* does not permit. The Buddhists account of self, thus, does not have any fitting in the agent-cause paradigm of action.

The Sāṁkhya account of *kartā* also does not seem to be satisfactory and sensible. Because the Sāṁkhya notion of self (*puruṣa*) does not satisfy the logical requirements of *karma.* Though Sāṁkhya believes in a permanent conscious self, but the self of Sāṁkhya does not satisfy the criterion of a *kartā*. For the self in Sāṁkhya philosophy is regarded as inactive (*akartā*). Though *prakṛti* is regarded as a *kartā* of *karma* but *prakṛti* being unconscious cannot play the role of a *kartā*. Because actions are conscious phenomena, which cannot be the product of any unconscious cause. Moreover, actions are purposive in nature, and purposive actions, cannot be conceived to have their origin from the unconscious cause. An unconscious matter cannot carry out the processes of action. It does not have the capacity to choose or to decide which a purposive action requires for its origination. Thus in admitting that there is a purposive action but denying at the same time the existence of a conscious actor, the Sāṁkhya commits itself to an absurd position, because unconscious teleology is unintelligible.[3] Therefore, the Sāṁkhya account of self *(puruṣa)* and matter *(prakṛti)* do not have any fitting in the agent-cause paradigm of action. In fact, the Sāṁkhya system does not maintain any distinction between *kartā* and cause, action and event like Buddhism.

The Nyāya-Vaiśeṣika, account of *kartā* also does not satisfy the logical requirements of *karma.* Nyāya- Vaiśeṣika believes in two types of *kartā* : finite *kartā* *(jīva)* and infinite *kartā* (God). But both the finite and infinite selves do not satisfy the logical requirements of *karma.* The finite self in Nyāya-Vaiśeṣika is regarded as unconscious *(jaḍa)*. Consciousness is said is the accidental quality of the self. But an unconscious self cannot play the role of a *kartā* . Because *karma* is a conscious phenomenon, which always presupposes a conscious agent. Therefore, the Nyāya-Vaiśeṣika account of finite self *(jīva)* cannot play the role of a *kartā.* Like finite *kartā* *(jīva)*, infinite *kartā.* (God) also does not satisfy the logical conditions of *karma* because Nyāya- Vaiśeṣika conceives God as disembodied and the concept of *kartṛtva* (agency) presupposes the involvement of body and bodily movements. This we have already seen. A disembodied being cannot become the *kartā* of *karma.* So God, on this account, cannot play the role of a *kartā.* Thus Nyāya- Vaiśeṣika theories of finite and infinite selves do not have any fitting in the agent-cause paradigm of action.

Prabhākara Mīmāṁsakas also do not give a satisfactory account of *kartā.* Because Prabhākara Mīmāṁsakas, like Nyāya-Vaiśeṣika, hold that the self is essentially unconscious *(jaḍa)* and consciousness is its only an accidental quality which may or may not be possessed by the soul. But an unconscious substance cannot become the agent of any action, a conscious phenomenon. Over and above, purposive actions cannot be said to be the product of any unconscious thing. Therefore the self of Prabhākara Mīmāṁsakas also does not have any fitting in the agent-cause paradigm of action.

Among all the classical Indian schools of philosophy, only the Vedānta and the Jaina view of *kartā* seems to be satisfactory. Because, according to Vedānta and Jainism, human self is in the nature of consciousness. It possesses the power of activity. It is a substantial being which a sensible theory of *karma* requires.

Notes and References

1. Eliot Deutsch, *Advaita Vedānta*, The University Press of Hawaii, Honolulu, 1973, p. 68.
2. MacMurray, '*What is Action*?", Proceedings of the Aristotelian Society, Suppl. xvii (1938).
3. Datta and Chatterjee, *An Introduction to Indian Philosophy*, University of Calcutta, Eighth Edition, 1984, p. 363.

3

Karma and Karma Phala

In the preceding chapter we analysed the notions of *kartā* and *karma.* And while analysing the notions of *kartā* and *karma* we had seen that the notions of *kartā* and *karma* are conceptually connected. The notion of *kartā* , like the notion of *karma,* has no meaning in isolation. It is a functional notion and not a referential notion whose meaning can be understood apart from and independent of the notion of activity (*kriyā*). Its meaning consists in activity and activity has no meaning outside the context of action. Activity and action are conceptually connected. Activity involves in it the notion of process and action is the end of that process. Activity without action is not possible and action without activity is not conceivable. Both are inter-related concepts. The notion of *karma* essentially involves in it the notion of a conscious agency in the sense that without conscious agency no *karma* is possible. For to be a *kartā* or an agent, one must have the sense of agency, the sense that he can do something. It is the *kartā* who makes action possible. But the *kartā* is not a *kartā* without *karma. Karma* is different from event. The notion of event does not essentially involve in it the notion of conscious agency who makes an event to happen. But the notion of *karma* essentially involves in it the notion of a conscious agency. In fact, it is the involvement of the conscious agency that distinguishes action from event. Events occur when certain antecedent conditions are present. Events are not done. They just happen when certain antecedent conditions are present. But actions are done and doing always involves a reference to somebody who brings action into effect. They just do not happen when certain antecedent conditions are present. They are always brought about through conscious activities and efforts. From this point of view, we can say that actions are conscious phenomena unlike events. Actions are purposive in character. They are willed, planned and pursued. But events are neither intended nor aimed. They cannot be said to be purposive in character. Material things and events cannot play the role of a *kartā* nor the notion of a *kartā* can be analysed in terms of them. This, however, does not mean that *karma* is possible without the involvement of body and bodily movements. No *karma* is possible without the involvement of bodily movements. But body and bodily movements cannot by themselves, given their nature, produce action. Because actions are of such kind that they can be either done or undone. They can be performed or refrained which neither material body nor even its bodily movements can do. Only conscious beings can be said to have power to bring about action or to refrain from it. This is the reason why only a conscious being can legitimately be said to be the *kartā* of *karma* and none else. Agent's beliefs, attitudes, intentions, cognitions, desires, passions, motives and circumstances no doubt may play causal roles in certain respects in the production of action but none of these elements can be assigned with the role of a *kartā* since they lack agential characteristics. For to be a doer, the doer must have a body. Without body the doer ceases to be a doer. Since only a conscious being with body can act or be the agent of action, or even be acted upon, the self itself cannot do any action or be the object of any action being disembodied. A living being i.e., human being who is an embodied self can and does act. Passions, emotions etc. which are generally regarded as psychological factors and move us to do certain actions are essentially associated with the body and not with the self. Like disembodied self, God also does not fulfil the logical requirements of an action. God cannot perform action because He has no body. Only an embodied being can perform action. But to say this does not mean that body by itself can initiate action. Body cannot by itself initiate action though it is causally connected. Actions occur when embodied conscious being causes them. If embodied conscious being does not execute his power, action cannot come into effect. And only a conscious being who can do something can have sense of doing. A non-agent cannot have a sense of doing nor can it be acted upon. Since only conscious beings can act, and be acted upon, they can be said to be the doer of action.

If the notion of *karma* is conceptually different from the notion of event then the *phala* of *karma* (the result and/or consequence of action) cannot be said to be identical with the *phala* of event (or the effect of event). Both are conceptually different. All cases of *karma phala* are the cases of *event phala* since they are caused by *karma* and *karma* is a kind of event because it is caused by a *kartā* through the association of body and bodily movements. But all cases of *event phala* are not the cases of *karma phala* because they are all not caused by *karma.* They are caused by events. And events do not essentially involve in them the notion of any conscious agency which the notion of *karma* does. Since *karma phala* is essentially connected with *karma* and *karma* is essentially connected with *kartā, karma phala* is not conceivable without *kartā* and *karma. Kartā* and *karma* are necessary and sufficient conditions for *karma phala* to happen. But these are not the antecedent conditions of *event phala.* That is because the *phala* of event does not essentially involve in it a reference to *karma* and *kartā* . *Event phalas* can be conceived apart from and independent of *karma* and *kartā* because events from where *event phalas* originate are conceivable apart from and independent of them. The notion of event (or effect) is conceptually connected with the notion of cause in the sense that without cause, no event can happen, and the notion of cause is different from the notion of *kartā* (this we have already seen in the second chapter). This is the reason why causal events cannot be held to be morally responsible and accountable for their effects. In fact, the notion of deserving, accountability and responsibility do not have any meaningful applicability in the domain of events. They do have meaningful applicability only in the domain of *kartā* who can act and be acted upon; and only one who can act and be acted upon can be held to be morally responsible and accountable for whatever he does, good or bad. Events do not, and cannot, perform actions and hence cannot be held to be morally responsible and accountable for their effects. The notion of *event phala,* thus, is conceptually dissociated from the notions of deserving, accountability and responsibility from which the notion of *karma phala* is not dissociated. The reason why *karma phala* is not dissociated from the notions of deserving, accountability and responsibility is that *karma phala* is connected with *karma* and *karma* is associated with *kartā* who performs *karma* and only one who performs *karma* can legitimately be held to be morally responsible and accountable for what he does, good or bad. *Karma phala* and *event phala*, thus, do not fall under the same logical category, though *karma phala* is also a kind of *phala* (effect).

To say that *karma phala* without *karma* and *kartā* is not possible is not to say that *karma* and *kartā* cannot ontologically exist without *karma phala*. *Karma* and *kartā* are conceivable without *karma phala* because the latter does not form a part of the meaning of the former. All *karmas* may not yield *karma phala*. They may be abortive. This is not only logically but also factually quite possible. Action as event can be conceived to exist without causing another event as its *phala* but no *event phala* can be conceived to happen without being caused. Besides, the notions of *karma* and *kartā* always come logically prior to the notion of *karma phala* and what comes logically prior to something cannot be said to be grounded in it. If this be so, *karma* and *kartā* can be conceived to exist apart from and independent of *karma phala*. But this does not, however, mean that they are not causally connected. *Karma phala* is causally connected with *karma* and *karma* is causally connected with *kartā* . Though the process of producing *karma phala* remains as causal but the *karmic* process involves something more over and above the process of producing *karma phala*, that is, judging, evaluating, deliberating and choosing on the account of which the notions of reward and punishment in the forms of pleasure and pain are attached to *karma phala*. An action is individuated by reference to the intended result and intended result of action is different from that of its actual result. And both the results may or may not coincide. Every action has its reaction in one or the other form and reaction of an action can be said to be its result. But this notion of result is quite different from that of the intended one and both the notions of result must not be confused. The notion of *karma phala* when we use it, we do not use it in the sense of reaction of action because the notion of reaction does not distinguish the notion of *karma phala* from the notion of *event phala*. Because *event phala* is also the result or the reaction of another event. *Karma phala* is an intended result of *karma* which is desired and brought about through conscious activities and efforts, although in doing so a *kartā* may or may not get success. This is perfectly quite possible because success and unsuccess are two dimensions of an action. A *kartā* has no control over the actual result of an action. He has control only over action and action alone which he performs to attain the desired end. And in so doing an action may or may not bring the intended result. The actual result may not coincide with the intended one. Since the *kartā* has no control over the actual result of an action, he cannot be held to be responsible on that account. He can neither be condemned nor even commended from the moral point of view. He can be held to be responsible on the account of his action, not the result of his action. But when we say that the intended result of an action is different from that of its actual result is not to say that intended result of action cannot be the actual result of action. Intended result of action can also be the actual result of action. Because both notions of result are not mutually incompatible though are logically unrelated. This is the reason why what is intended may also be that which is actual. But the coincidence between the two, if at all it exists, will be there as a matter of fact, not as a matter of logic. The intention with which an action is done may be positive or negative in the sense that a *kartā* may do certain action in order to get something or to avoid the occurrence of something. Either way his action is intentional since it is done with intention. Sometimes a distinction is made between intention and desire. But here we do not make any distinction between the two and use them synonymously. It is sometimes debated whether the concept of intention or desire is logically involved in the concept of action. But we shall not go into this issue here. Normally the notion of action does involve in it the notion of desire or intention of one or the other kind which makes obligatory for the doer to experience some happiness or sorrow. One cannot exhaust experiencing all that he has to on account of his action in the same life in which they have been done. Therefore he has to be reborn after his death to experience the unexperienced result of his action. The upholders of the doctrine of *karma* do not make the sharp distinction between the intended and actual result of *karma*. They muddled both the notions of result i.e., actual and intended in their conception of *karma phala*. According to their account, *karma phala* of *karma* may be either in the form of impressions or tendencies, or in the forms of pleasure and pain which are treated, according to them, as a kind of reward and punishment respectively which the doer of *karma* is believed to reap sooner or later either in the present life or the life after death. However, whatever the *karma phala* may be whether they are intended or unintended; whether they first produce impressions and tendencies which consequently produce pleasure and pain according to their nature or not, they are all said to be the result of *karma.* Without *karma* they cannot happen. They can be stopped only by stopping *karmas* because they are produced by them. Happiness and pain which are treated by the upholders of the doctrine of *karma* as a kind of reward and punishment may vary in degree according to the nature of *karma* and its accumulated impressions.

If *karma* as an event is ontologically possible to exist without necessarily producing *karma phala,* the *karma* does not cease to be a *karma* when it does not produce its intended result. The *karma* remains as a *karma* regardless of its intended *phala.* So the *phala* of *karma* cannot function as a criterion to decide whether something is *karma* or not. The *karma* is a *karma* not because it produces *karma phala* but because it is done through conscious activities and efforts. It is intended and brought about by the *kartā.* Likewise, the *kartā* is not a *kartā* because whatever he does, does produce intended result but because he does action. If *karma* and *kartā* were logically rested on *karma phala,* there would have been no possibility of conceiving them apart from and independent of *karma phala.* But since it is possible to conceive them apart from and independent of *karma phala;* they cannot be said to be grounded in *karma phala.* In fact, it is not the *karma* and the *kartā* which are dependent on the *karma phala* but it is the *karma phala* which is dependent on them in the sense that without *karma* and *kartā, karma phala* cannot be conceived to happen. It is the *karma* of *kartā* that makes *karma phala* possible. *Karma* and *kartā* both are necessary and sufficient conditions to produce *karma phala.* To say that *karma phala* without *karma* is not conceivable is not to say that *karma phala* regularly follows from *karma.* It only means that no *karma phala* can come into existence without *karma* and to say this does not amount to mean that *karma phala* regularly follows from *karma. Karma phala* may or may not regularly follow from *karma* since its relation with *karma* is contingent. Not only this, the same *karma phala* may follow from different *karmas,* and the same *karma* may produce different results in different contexts. This is possible because the relation between action and its result is a causal. An action does not guarantee that it will have the same set of results in all circumstances. What sorts of result an action will be producing cannot be determined by the rules of logic. It can be determined only after empirical investigation. So even if *karma* is done, *karma phala* may not follow, and if it follows, it may not follow regularly. *Karma* does not necessitate *karma phala.* If this view is correct, it is quite obvious that the *kartā* may remain as a *kartā* even when his *karma* does not produce *karma phala* regularly or irregularly and not vice-versa. *Karma phala* without *karma* and *kartā* is not conceivable but *karma* and *kartā* are conceivable without *karma phala.* That is possible because *karma* and *kartā* are not ontologically grounded in *karma phala.* The relation of *kartā* and *karma* with *karma phala* thus, is not a reciprocal or two directional relation. It is one directional relation. If *karma* without *karma phala* is possible, then the context in which *karma* does not produce *karma phala* we cannot say that the *kartā* does reap the result of whatever he does since whatever he does, does not necessarily produce the result. So the question of a *kartā's* being getting the result of his *karma* does arise only when his *karma* produces its result. The context in which *karma* does not produce any result the question of *kartā's* being getting the result of it simply does not arise. It also does not arise in the context in which no action is performed positively or negatively. Reaping of the *karma phala* of *karma* is quite a different from that of producing it. Both the notions should not be confused because to produce is not to reap and to reap is not to produce. Two are logically unconnected notions. Saying this does not amount to mean that they are incompatible notions. Both the notions are not incompatible notions. They can go together. Therefore factually, though not logically, it is quite possible that the *kartā* of *karma* may also be that who is the *bhoktā* (experiencer) of *karma phala. Karma phala* becomes inevitable only when it is presupposed that the *kartā* of *karma* is also a *bhoktā* of *karma phala* of that *karma*. Unless we presuppose it, we cannot say that we reap whatever we sow which the doctrine of *karma* states. Because what makes *karma phala* inevitable is the relationship of *kartā* and *bhoktā* with *karma phala.* If the *kartā* is not related to the *karma phala* of *karma* by way of a *bhoktā,* the *karma phala* of that *karma* cannot be said to be inevitable. The thesis of inevitability of *karma phala* does hold only when we assume that the *kartā* of *karma* is also a *bhoktā* of *karma phala* of that *karma,* or else it becomes fallible. The notions of *kartā* and *bhoktā* are conceptually different and unconnected. They are not related to the *karma phala* in the same way. *Karma* is causally related to *kartā* in the sense that without *kartā* no *karma* can happen and without *karma* nobody can be said to be the *kartā.* The *kartā* can remain as a *kartā* of *karma* even if he does not experience *karma phala* of his *karma.* But the relation of *bhoktā* and *karma phala* is a relation of the enjoyer and enjoyed. Somebody becomes the *bhoktā* of *karma phala* when he realizes it, which need not be the *karma phala* of any of his *karma.* The *kartā* plays an active role in bringing about the result of action. Without *kartā* no result of action can happen. But the *bhoktā* does not play any active role in bringing about the *karma phala* of *karma.* So he cannot be said to be the cause of *karma phala.* He may receive the *karma phala* even without playing any causal or non-causal role in its production. And to receive *karma phala* is not to cause *karma phala* and to cause *karma phala* is not to receive it. Causing and receiving notions are different and logically unconnected, though they are quite compatible. Since to cause is not to receive and to receive is not to cause, somebody may receive some *karma phala* which may not be *karma phala* of any of his action or somebody may produce some *karma phala* through his actions and yet he may not receive *karma phala* of his *karma.* In other words, the *kartā* may not be a *bhoktā* and the *bhoktā* may not be a *kartā* of the same *karma phala.* This is perfectly conceivable because the notion of *kartṛtva* does not essentially involve in it the notion of *bhoktṛtva.* And the notion of *bhoktṛtva* does not essentially involve in it the notion of *kartṛtva. Kartṛtva* and *bhoktṛtva* notions taken in isolation do not rule out the logical possibility of *kṛtapraṇāśa* and *akṛtābhyāgama prasaṅgas*. Above all, the notion of *kartā* is essentially connected with the notion of *karma,* but the notion of *bhoktā* is not essentially connected with the notion of *karma.* The notion of *bhoktā* is essentially connected with the notion of *karma phala* with which the notion of *kartā* is not essentially connected. Therefore confusing the notion of *kartā* with that of *bhoktā* and thinking that they are related with *karma phala* in the same way would be tantamount to committing a mistake. But when the *kartā* is also conceived as a *bhoktā* of *karma phala* of *karma,* that is, when the *kartā* is related to the *karma phala* by way of a *bhoktā,* the *karma phala* becomes inevitable. It rules out the logical possibility of anybody's getting some result which is not the result of any of his action. *Kartā-bhoktā - karma phala* relation binds the *kartā* to realize the *karma phala* of his *karma* sooner or later during his present life or life after death. But any *karma* paradigm which presupposes *kartā - bhoktā -karma phala* relation is bound to be agent-centric, self-centric and monistic in character, because it attributes everything good or bad, one has or will ever have to only one kind of causes i.e., to his and only his actions. But experience does not seem to support it. Not only this, it also makes moral, religious and socio-cultural interpersonal actions impossible because moral, socio-cultural and religious interpersonal actions involve a reference to some other beings for whom actions are performed.

But in *kartā - bhoktā—karma phala* paradigm of *karma* the *kartā* can be a *bhoktā* only when it is presupposed that the *kartā* and the *bhoktā* signify one and the same conscious being who exists and persists through different times and have powers of *kartṛtva* and *bhoktṛtva* and the *karma phala* of *karma* does not perish before the realization by its doer. No embodied conscious being can be both the *kartā* and the *bhoktā,* if he does not possess the characteristics of *kartṛtva* and *bhoktṛtva* which would not be possible without his being existing and persisting at different times. It would also not be possible, if the *karma phala* of *karma* is destroyed before its realization. *Kartā - bhoktā—karma phala* relation, thus, necessitates not only that the *kartā* and the *bhoktā* must be identical but also the conservability of *karma phala.* Unless we presuppose the identity of *kartā* and *bhoktā* and the conservability of *karma phala* till its realization, we cannot say that an action entitles its doer to some joys or sorrows which he unfailingly gets what he is entitled to or deserves. This implies that if the *kartā* does no persist at different times, he cannot realize the *karma phala* of his *karma* and in that case *kṛtapraṇāśa* (a situation where one performs an action but does not realize its fruit) is bound to happen and the *kartā* cannot be a *bhoktā* of *karma phala* of his *karma* which *kartā - bhoktā—karma phala* paradigm of *karma* requires. If the *kartā* is not a *bhoktā,* then someone may get some result which may not be the result of any of his action. And in that case *akṛtābhyāgama prasaṅga* (a situation where one is led to some result which is not the result of any of his action) is bound to occur. Therefore to avoid unhappy moral situations of *kṛtapraṇāśa* and *akṛtābhyāgama* we have to presuppose not only some amount of the stability and permanency of *kartā* but also to admit that the *kartā* is also a *bhoktā* and the *karma phala* of *karma* is not destroyed before its realization. Morality involving the notions of justice, responsibi-lity and accountability requires that each human being should reap only the fruit of his own action, not of the others. Any version of the doctrine of *karma* which does not assume the identity of *kartā* and *bhoktā* and the conservability of *karma phala* is bound to be unsatisfactory and morally unintelligible. It cannot explain different occurrences of human life satisfactorily for which it is designed. The rejection of either of the presuppositions mentioned above makes the doctrines of transmigration of *saṁskāras* and soul impossible. No doubt, *kartā-bhoktā-karma phala* paradigm of *karma* is coherent and viable and establishes that man is the maker of his own fate. He himself is the cause of his sufferings and unhappiness and no one else nor can he be the cause of others sufferings. But it rules out a genuine human concern for others which forms an integral part of our moral social consideration.

Even if we presuppose the identity of *kartā bhoktā* and the conservability of *karma phala* of *karma,* it does not follow from it that the doer of good gets good results and the doer of bad gets bad results and no doer gets a reverse result of any of his actions unless we further presuppose that *karma* produces its fitting result, that is, good action produces good result and bad action produces bad result and no good action produces bad result or bad action produces good result under any condition. When we make all these presuppositions then and then alone we can legitimately say that the doer of good gets good results and the doer of bad gets bad results and no doer gets a reverse result of his actions. A man reaps what he sows and he can be good by doing good deeds and bad by doing bad deeds. But these *karmic* assertions cannot be validated on the empirical grounds. Nor can they be said to be the result of inductive generalization from a set of empirical data. They are neither provable nor refutable by means of any evidence obtained from experience. It would not, therefore, be fair to make use of any pro-and-con empirical evidence in assessing its acceptability or validity. The intelligibility of the doctrine of *karma* and its assertions depend upon their internal coherence. And when we examine from this point of view, we find that monistic explanation of the doctrine of *karma* is morally intelligible and satisfactory doctrine though experience does not support it. Because in experience we find that in many cases a man suffers not due to any action of his own but due to hostile action of others or due to some other natural events i.e., earthquake, floods etc. Likewise, in many cases it is also seen that a man enjoys not because of any action of his own but because of others action. Even if it is admitted that whatever man gets, gets because of his action, we cannot establish it scientifically. It always remains a matter of belief, not as a matter of logic or fact. Monistic or self-centric interpretation of the doctrine of *karma* is inconsistent with its theistic interpretation, because according to the theistic version of the doctrine of *karma, karma* always requires a moral administrator of the world, who is none other than God which monistic interpretation of the doctrine of *karma* rules out. According to the monistic interpretation of the doctrine of *karma,* man gets whatever he does on the account of his own deeds irrespective of the roles of others, divine or human being. Reward and punishment automatically follow as a consequence of his action without the involvement of any divine power. It does not admit the assumption of any moral administrator over and above the *karmic* process. Reward and punishment in the forms of happiness and pain are built in its structure. It traces all suffering to the agent and removes bitterness against God or neighbour as Hiriyanna rightly observes.[1] But in the monistic *karmic* world, the notions of reward and punishment are used in technical sense, not in ordinary sense. In ordinary sense the notions of reward and punishment not only involve a reference to happiness and pain respectively but also a reference to some other conscious being who evaluates goodness or badness of an action done by the doer according to certain norms and awards reward and punishment accordingly to him which the monistic theory that is, *kartā-bhokta-karma phala* paradigm of *karma,* does not admit. On the monistic interpretation of the doctrine of *karma,* the doer gets reward and punishment in the forms of happiness and pain respectively on the account of what he owes by his deeds and deeds alone, without the involvement of any external agency which the ordinary conceptions of reward and punishment involve. "But the concept of a consequence and that of a reward or punishment are not of the same logical type, since the former is causal, empirical, while the latter is normative or evaluative."[2] *Karma phala* has both a causal and an evaluative components in it and both the components must not be confused. *Karma phala* has a causal component because it causally results from the causal *karmic* process, and it has an evaluative component because the *karmic* process from which it results, involves judging, evaluating, decision making etc. on the account of which he merits reward and punishment. Reward and punishment vary according to the nature of *karma.* Monistic interpretation of the doctrine of *karma* provides us incentive or motivation because it states that man reaps what he sows, which non-monistic interpretation of *karma* does not provide. Man deserves *karma phala* not because of its utility or disutility but because of his *karma.* It is the *karma* which entitles its doer to owe the *phala* of it, good or bad. In this respect we can say that the monistic account of *karma* is different from the utilitarian account, according to which what one deserves is determined by the consequences of his actions. But when we attempt to know whether so and so really did such and such action in the past on the account of which he is getting such and such consequence in life, we face trouble because past actions to which consequences are related can never be known and established on the empirical grounds. It always remains as a matter of belief, not as a matter of fact. An action produces result not because it is done by this or that desire, or it is moral or immoral; or it is religious or non-religious etc. but because of its being an action. The *karma phala* is structurally built in the nature of action itself. But the action does not guarantee that it will have the same set of consequences in all circumstances, which the monistic account of the doctrine of *karma* presupposes.

From the foregoing analysis it is quite evident that no classical Indian account of the doctrine of *karma* i.e., Buddhism, Jainism and Hinduism can be said to be consistent and coherent. They all suffer from one or the other weakness. For example, Buddhism denies substantial existence of being, conscious and unconscious and holds the theories of momentariness (*kṣaṇabhaṅgavāda*) and impermanency (*anityatā*). But a momentary and impermanent self, on their account, cannot experience the fruit of his action since the agent vanishes before the emergence of result. Even if it is admitted that the agent lasts and possesses some amount of stability and constancy, he may not get the fruit of his action, because the result of action, on their account, is perishable before its realization. Not only this, it can even go to some other individual, according to the Buddhist doctrine. Which means, an individual can be led to some result which need not be the result of any of his actions. The Buddhists account of *karma,* thus, suffers from the fallacies of *kṛtapraṇāśa* and *akṛtābhyāgama* and therefore it does not have any fitting in the *kartā - bhoktā -karma phala* paradigm of *karma.*

In the Sāṁkhya system, the *puruṣa* (self) being an inactive cannot be regarded as a *kartā*. He does not perform action but he is regarded as a *bhoktā* which is inconsistent with the self-centric doctrine of *karma. Prakṛti* performs action but does not reap the result of her action, which violates the basic principle of the theory of *karma.* The Sāṁkhya account of *karma* does not have any fitting in the *kartā - bhoktā—karma phala* paradigm of *karma* since it suffers from the fallacies of *kṛtapraṇāśa,* and *akṛtābhyāgama*.

In the Nyāya-Vaiśeṣika system, God is regarded as a *kartā* in the sense that He creates the world process and administers the law of *karma.* But He is not regarded as a *bhoktā* of his *karma* which goes against the self-centric doctrine of *karma.* Because according to the self-centric doctrine of *karma,* one who performs action irrespective of its nature, reaps the result of *karma,* if the *karma* produces result. *Kartā* is not conceived over and above the *karmic* process. But in the theistic system, like Nyāya-Vaiśeṣika and Viśiṣṭādvaita, God is conceived over and above the *karmic* process. He is conceived as a *kartā* but is not regarded as a *bhoktā* of his *karma phala.* On their accounts, God performs actions but He is not touched by the effects of actions which is inconsistent with the *karmic* assertions in the *kartā - bhoktā -karma phala* paradigm of *karma.*

According to the Mīmāṁsaka schools of thought, obligatory actions, when they are violated, yield results but when they are performed, do not yield any result. This view of action does not go along with the assertions of the doctrine of *karma,* because according to the doctrine of *karma,* yielding of the result of *karma* does not depend upon its violation or conformation but upon its performance. If violation of an action can yield some result, conformation to that action can also, on the same ground, yield some result. The Mīmāṁsā view of *karma* does not have any fitting in the *kartā - bhoktā -karma phala* paradigm of *karma.*

According to the Hindu *vedic* system of thought, every individual has to pay off the following debts (*riṇa*) : (1) *Devariṇa,* debt to the gods for the invaluable gifts of air, fire, water, food etc. In lieu of these gifts we have to make some offerings of our own to the gods who control nature as tokens of our gratitude. (2) *Pitririṇa,* debt to the parents for their having given birth to us and having brought us up. *Pitririṇa* is also called *śrāddha.* In *śrāddha* ceremony the ritualistic offerings are given by the son to his parents in order to help his deceased parents in their abode after death. (3) *Riṣiriṇa,* debt to the teachers, discoverers and inventors who have brought civilization to this stage and to whom we owe our knowledge. The concept of *yajña* is a later development of the concept of *riṇa.* According to the Hindu *vedic* system of thought, there are five kinds of *yajñas* or 'sacrifices'. They are : (1) *Devayajña,* offerings to the gods or the powers which control nature and its various phenomena. (2) *Riṣiyajña,* offerings to the great seers and sages who have advanced civilization and culture and have given wisdom. (3) *Pitriyajña,* offerings to the ancestors and parents. (4) *Bhūtayajña,* offerings to all the creatures of the world, and (5) *nriyajña,* offerings to the fellow human beings. But the Hindu *vedic* conceptions of *riṇa* and *yajña* are not consistent with the *karmic* assertions in the *kartā - bhoktā -karma phala* paradigm of *karma,* because according to the theory of *kartā - bhoktā -karma phala* paradigm of *karma,* the fruits of action accrue to those who actually perform action and not to those for whom actions are performed. While according to the Hindu *vedic* system of thought, the fruits of action accrue not to those who actually perform it (i.e., *ritvik*), but to him who has paid them to perform the action (*yajamāna*). Not only this, it is also said that one who does not perform the action also gets the results of action. For example, the result of *śrāddha* offered by the son to help his deceased parents in their abode after death is believed goes to his deceased parents who do not perform actually the acts of *śrāddha*.

Not only the *Vedic* conceptions of *riṇa* and *yajña* but the *Upaniṣadic* description of *karma* also does not seem to have any fitting in the monistic and self-centric paradigm of *karma,* because the *Upaniṣads* propound the view that the son takes over the actions of the father.[3] In the *Śāntiparva*[4] and the *Manusmriti*[5], also, there is mention of the *karma* of the forefather affecting the children. Manu says that punishment strikes down the king who swerves from his duty, together with his relatives.[6] Again, it is stated that a faithful wife shares the fate of her husband.[7] According to the *Manicarajātaka* (*Jātaka* no. 194) famines, floods etc. are brought about by the faults of the King.[8] These views of *karma* do not have any fitting in the *kartā - bhoktā -karma phala* paradigm of *karma.* All these views suffer from one or the other weakness, and go against the monistic and self-centric doctrine of *karma.* Although the monistic and self-centric doctrine of *karma* is a consistent doctrine but it is not free from the philosophical problems. There are a lot of problems connected with the theory of *karma phala.* For example, where and how is the *karma phala* of *karma* stored to be realized by its doer in subsequent of time ? Regarding this question, the *karmavādins* have different opinions. Those who do not believe in the existence of God seem to advocate the view that the *karma phala* is stored in the individual's soul who performs *karma.* But how does it reside in the agent's soul and in what form does it reside ? Regarding these questions we do not find any satisfactory answer from them. Those who believe in the existence of God and conceive Him as the moral administrator of the world maintain the view that the *karma phala* of *karma* is stored by God and when the time comes He dispenses it to its doer. But when the question is asked : Why does He do it? Does He do it out of his kindness? If so, in what form and where does He store the *karma phala* of *karma* ? Regarding these questions again we do not find any satisfactory explanation from the theists. Moreover, God is conceived by the theists as disembodied and the disembodied existence of an agent on our analysis of the theory of *karma* is not possible at all. If this be the case, how can God be said to be the storer of merits and demerits of our actions as the theistic *karmavādins* believe. Even those *karmavādins* who believe in the monistic and self-centric conception of the doctrine of *karma* do not seem to hold a consistent view. For example, if birth is determined by *karma,* as they say, then it must be accepted that the one who takes birth had performed some *karmas* before his birth which is absurd. Because *karmas* cannot be performed before birth. The ontological existence of an individual always comes logically prior to his performance of *karmas*. If this is so, then *karma* cannot be said to be the cause of birth of an individual. And if it is the cause of the birth of any individual, it cannot be said to be the *phala* of his birth. Both the statements one cannot hold consistently. But since both the theistic and non-theistic *karmavādins* hold both the statements together, their accounts of *karma* cannot be said to be self-consistent.

Notes and References

1. Rajendra Prasad, *Karma Causation and Retributive Morality,* Munshiram Manoharlal Publishers Pvt. Ltd., New Delhi, 1989, p. 225.
2. *Ibid.*, p. 227.
3. *Brihadāraṇyaka*, 1,5,17 and *Kauṣṭaki* II, 15.
4. *Śāntiparva* 1, 29.
5. *Manusmriti* IV, 170.
6. *Manu*, vii, 28.
7. *Manu*, V. 166, ix. 29.
8. E. W. Hopkins, *"Modification of the karma doctrine"*, *Journal of Royal Asiatic Society,* 1906, pp. 581-593.

4

Karma : Freedom and Responsibility

In the preceding chapter we analysed the concepts of *karma*, *karma phala* and their relation. By way of analysis we find out that *kartā* and *karma* are not ontologically dependent on *karma phala* because they are conceivable without *karma phala.* But *karma phala* is not conceivable without *kartā* and *karma.* Its existence always presupposes the existence of *kartā* and *karma.* Over and above, the *karma* does not necessitate the *karma phala.* The *karma* is abortive in character. Because of this it is quite possible that the *kartā* may remain as a *kartā* even when his *karma* does not produce *karma phala* (intended result) and when his *karma* does not produce *karma phala,* the *kartā* does not reap the result of whatever he does. Therefore, it is quite possible that the *kartā* may remain as a *kartā* even without reaping the result of his action. Reaping the *karma phala* of *karma* is different from that of producing it. Both the notions are logically unconnected, though are quite compatible. The notions of *kartā* and *bhoktā* are conceptually different and logically unconnected. They are not related to *karma phala* in the same way. The *kartā* plays an active role in bringing about the result of action, but the *bhoktā* may not play any active role so far the production of *karma phala* of *karma* is concerned. He may receive *karma phala* even without playing any active role in its production. Since the *kartā* and the *bhoktā* are related differently to the *karma phala* and are not logically connected, it is quite possible that the *kartā* may not be a *bhoktā* and the *bhoktā* may not be a *kartā* of the same *karma phala.* The notion of *karta* is conceptually connected with the notion of *karma,* while the notion of *bhoktā* is conceptually connected with the notion of *karma phala.* This is the reason why it is quite possible that the *kartā* may not be a *bhoktā* and the *bhoktā* may not be a *kartā*. But to accept this line of thought goes against the doctrine of *karma,* because in that case, it would suffer from the fallacies of *kṛtapraṇās'a,* and *akṛtābhyāgama* which a sound theory of *karma* does not allow. A sound theory of *karma,* as we have already seen, always requires the identity of *kartā* and *bhoktā.* When *kartā* and *bhoktā* are treated as one and the same entity or taken in identical sense the fallacies of *kṛtapraṇāśa,* and *akṛtābhyāgama* do not arise and the theory of *karma* becomes logically and morally sound. But when we relate the notion of *kartā* to the notion of *karma phala* by way of a *bhoktā*, the question naturally arises: Can we hold him responsible for whatsoever *karma phala* he realizes? Surely not. Because a *kartā* can be held to be responsible for the *karma phala* of his *karma* only when he performs his *karma* freely. If he does not do his action freely, he cannot be held responsible for the *karma phala* of his *karma* which he gets. In other words, we cannot say that the *kartā* is responsible for his action and he deserves whatever he gets unless it is presupposed that whatever he did, he did it freely. The notion of responsibility is essentially connected with the notion of free action, not merely with action and it is the notion of free action which makes the notion of responsibility meaningful and intelligible. Denial of freedom contradicts responsibility and makes it meaningless and unintelligible. The notion of free action is a compound notion. It involves in it the notions of action and freedom. To identify it with anyone of them would amount to committing a mistake. Since the notion of responsibility is essentially connected with the notion of action, no one can be held responsible unless he performs action. This means that one who does not perform action cannot be held responsible for it. Only the agent can be held responsible. Material things and events which do not perform actions cannot be held responsible. In their contexts the notions of responsibility and accountability do not have any meaning. Such words do have meanings only in the context of the agent— cause paradigm of action. One who cannot do, cannot earn anything and one who cannot earn, cannot be said to be deserving of something. If something is not owned or earned by someone, he cannot be held to be deserving it. Since conscious beings i.e., human beings can do something, therefore they can earn something for which they can be held responsible. One who does not earn does not owe anything. And one who does not owe anything cannot be held to be deserving that thing, because he does not owe it. And if he does not owe anything, he cannot be held to be responsible for that thing. This means that only the agent can be said to be deserving something since he does something and thereby he earns. And what one earns, he owes it. And what he owes, he also deserves it.

Although it is true that no one can be held responsible unless he performs certain actions. But action is not the sole ground for holding him responsible, because the notion of responsibility is also essentially connected with the notion of freedom. Unless the agent's action is free, he cannot be held to be responsible for it and its result. The notion of freedom is an ambiguous notion. Generally, it is used in two different senses : Positive and negative.[1] In the negative sense, freedom refers to a condition characterized by the absence of coercion or constraint. In this sense, to be free means to be free from constraint or coercion imposed by internal or external factors whatsoever. In the positive sense, it refers to the possession of capacity or ability or power to do something. To be free in this sense means to have capacity or power to bring about certain actions or to make certain changes in the existing state of affairs. In Indian philosophy the notion of freedom although is used in both the senses, negative and positive, but it is used in the wider sense. In the negative sense, to be free means to be free from sufferings, pains and worldly existences, that is, mind, body and senses including *karmas* and not merely free from compulsions or constraints, internal or external. In the positive senses freedom means the attainment of self realization or identification of oneself with the absolute *(Advaita)* or the placement of the self in the company of God (*Viśiṣṭādvaita*) or acquisition of the state of pure-consciousness with awareness that it is distinct and different from everything *(kaivalya)* or the attainment of the highest good (*mokṣa*).

But in the context of *karma* we are using the word 'freedom' neither in the sense of freedom from sufferings and worldly existence nor in the sense of self-realization or acquisition of the state of pure consciousness with the awareness that it is distinct and different from everything else, as it has been used in Indian philosophy. We are using the word 'freedom' in the restricted sense. By 'freedom' here we mean not only the absence of certain conditions like constraint, coercion, innate incapacity, insanity, psychophysical disorders, ignorance etc., but also self-determination, self governance and self-control. In other words, the notion of freedom not only implies the absence of something i.e., constraints, hindrances, coercions, ignorance but also the presence of self-determination, self-governance and self-control. Therefore to say that the agent is free is to say that he himself determines, authorizes and imposes certain things i.e., rules, actions or prescriptions upon himself without any internal and or external enforcement or constraint of any sort. Freedom in the sense of 'freedom from' implies the absence or the negation of something and the absence or the negation of something always presupposes the existence of something. Unless something exists, the question of its negating does not arise. This means that unless there exist constraints or coercions, the question of their being getting eliminated or the agent's being free from them does not arise at all. The freedom of agent includes in its meaning not merely a 'freedom from' but a 'freedom to' as well. A freedom cannot be a freedom from in the context of action, if it is not also a freedom to. To free oneself from something or other is to make oneself free to do something or other. If there were no need to act freely, there would neither be any need to free oneself from restrictions. Freedom in the sense of 'freedom to' means to determine, to choose, to act, to impose or to play certain roles by himself without any internal or external enforcement. But to make oneself free from something or to do something always presupposes certain capacities i.e., choosing, imagining, deciding, reasoning , intending, understanding, deliberating, thinking, willing, desiring and making certain changes in the existing state of affairs. If someone has no capacity of making oneself free from or to do something; the concept of freedom cannot legitimately be applied to him. He cannot be said to have power to make oneself free from or to do something. But at the same time we must not forget that to have a power to make oneself free from or to do something is one thing and to exercise that power is another thing. If a person does not exercise his power to make himself free from or to do something, he cannot be said to be free even if he has potential power of doing it. In fact, we judge whether someone has potential power to make oneself free or not on the basis of his mental and physical activities. Exercising of the power of freedom is a conscious phenomenon which involves in it a reference to a conscious being. Exercising of the power of freedom being a conscious phenomenon cannot be said to have its origin from unconscious things or events like material bodies and psycho-physical events. No doubt, material things and events do have a power of causing certain things but they do not have power of making themselves free from or to do something. Only conscious beings can be conceived to have power to make themselves free. Therefore, the notion of freedom can be said to have its meaningful applicability in both the senses of freedom, that is, 'freedom from' and 'freedom to' only in the context of human conscious beings, not in the context of material things and events. Freedom of the agent not only presupposes the absence of something and to have capacity to do something but also the existence of the agent himself. Unless we presuppose that the agent exists, we cannot say that he has power of exercising freedom, nor can we say that he frees himself from something or other to do something or other. Freedom of choice consists in choosing between the alternatives whether to do this or to do that or whether to do or not to do. If there is no alternative, there exists no scope for choice; and if there is no scope for choice, there is no scope to act freely. A person acts freely when it is possible for him to act otherwise. Agent's free choice is controlled by the agent himself and not by any antecedent condition, divine or non-divine. While choosing of action it is quite possible that the agent may or may not be guided by certain rules and injunctions prescribed by the society or the scriptures. But when he chooses certain actions by himself without any constraint, internal or external, his action binds him to act accordingly whenever the situation arises provided the action is in his power to bring about. In this sense freedom implies self rule and self commitment. The primal mode of choice lies in the agent himself.

To be free is not to act arbitrarily. Freedom is different form arbitrariness. To be free in the context of choice means to form one's own opinion or judgement on certain questions and not to act arbitrarily. Freedom does not contradict self consistency which arbitrariness does. To be arbitrary means to be inconsistent. But to be free does not mean to be inconsistent. A free moral agent acts on principle and not without principle. Whereas an arbitrary agent does not act on any consistent principle. To act freely does not mean the absence of intentions, desires, beliefs, wants etc. Freedom is not opposed to intentions, desires, beliefs, choice, wants etc. while doing free action the agent may have certain beliefs, intentions, desires and wants etc. which may be causally responsible for the agent's performance of free action. Yet the causal roles of these are not incompatible with freedom. Freedom is opposed to constraints or compulsions, and to have certain beliefs, intentions, desires and wants is not necessarily to feel or to have constraints from them. To act freely means to choose, or to determine and control the action by himself without any enforcements. And to say this is not to say that there cannot be psycho-physical causal factors involved in the production of free action. No free action is possible without the involvement of bodily movement. But the bodily, movements do not arrest the freedom of the agent. In fact, the agent cannot exercise his power of freedom without the involvement of his body and bodily muscle constraints. So to be free is not to be bodiless, desireless, or unintentional. Freedom of choice consists in choosing between the different courses of action and in choosing so it is perfectly quite possible that the agent may be arbitrary or non-arbitrary, subjective or objective, right or wrong. Not only this, it is also quite possible that the agent may think or feel that he is free in choosing the alternatives and yet he may not be free due to the antecedent conditions which he himself does not know. He may be under illusion that he thinks he is free to choose. His freedom may be illusory. But under such situation if the agent does not know that he himself originates actions, he may not feel bound or compelled. Nor can he be held responsible for what he does. Freedom is opposed to ignorance.

From the foregoing discussions it is quite clear that the concept of responsibility we are using in the sense of self responsibility which is essentially connected with that of agent's autonomy or freedom. A self responsible person is one who is capable of making important decisions for himself. He is the sort of person who is capable of prescribing actions to himself and of conforming to them. A self responsible person is supposed to be capable of critical assessment and evaluation. He does not choose action simply because it has been prescribed by some authority, human or divine. To say this does not mean that he can never apply a principle without making a previous critical assessment. A self responsible person does not accept 'ready made' principles. He accepts what he thinks is right and in doing so he may be wrong. This is perfectly quite possible. A self responsible person not only chooses action freely but also sticks to what he chooses for himself. His commitment is implied by freedom and self responsibility. The concept of self responsibility is different from the other senses of responsibility, like capacity, accountability and role senses of responsibility. A person is said to be responsible in the capacity sense of responsibility, if he possesses certain capacities — understanding, reasoning, deciding, choosing, imagining, willing, desiring and intending etc., — the capacities which are considered as necessary for to be praised or blamed on the basis of his behaviour on certain particular occasions. The word 'accountability' generally is used in two senses : 'liability' and 'explicability'. The difference between 'explicability' and 'liability' lies in the fact that the former is mainly concerned with the acts and events, while the latter with the persons. The notion of liability, unlike the notion of explicability, presupposes the notion of a person. A person cannot be said to be responsible in the liable accountability sense of responsibility if he is not able of judging, deciding etc. This shows that liability sense of accountability is closely related to the capacity sense. But both the senses of responsibility are different. A person is said to be responsible in the accountability sense of responsibility for some action, if he or she is found to be answerable for them and not just because of the possession of certain capacities which it presupposes. A person is said to be responsible in the role sense of responsibility, if he does something in this or that role assigned to him. A person who does not perform the particular responsibility assigned to his role is called irresponsible. The concept of self responsibility is different from capacity, accountability and role sensess of responsibility in the sense that it is essentially connected with the autonomy of the individual with which the latter is not. The concept of self responsibility is closely related to the capacity, accountability and role senses of responsibility. A person cannot be said to be self responsible, if he or she is not endowed with the capacities of reasoning, understanding, judging, deciding , and choosing etc. Likewise, a person cannot be said to have self responsibility for some actions, if he or she is not found to be answerable for them. Not only this, he also cannot be said to be self responsible in the role sense of responsibility, if he or she does not perform this or that role which he or she assigns to himself or herself. A self responsible person is supposed to be one who is not only responsible for whatever he does freely i.e., actions but also what follows from his action i.e., *karma phala* (result of action). A free agent is responsible for the result of his action, good or bad. He owes what he does and what follows from his doing i.e., intended *karma* . And what he owes he must get it because he deserves it and whatever he deserves he is entitled to get it. This means that the notion of deserving is essentially connected with the notions of individual's freedom and responsibility. An occurrence over which a person had no control is something he cannot be held responsible for. Which means, in other words, a person can be held responsible for an occurrence over which he had control and not that which follows inevitably from his character, or any antecedent conditions. A person can be said to have control over action only if it is possible for him to do otherwise. Self responsibility always presupposes the agent's having control over the action. Agent's self actions should not be confused with events which inevitably follow from his character. By the 'agent's self action' we mean action that originates from the agent's self. The agent's self is not reducible to a bundle of dispositions. It has its own independent and distinct ontological existence. By 'the agent's character' we mean innate or acquired dispositions to behave in certain ways in particular circumstances which the agent's self may take into account while making a decision as to how to act but not being ruled by them.

There are three logical questions which are generally raised in connection with the notion of responsibility. They are : To whom is the notion of responsibility applicable ? On the account of what is so-and-so said responsible? What does so-and-so's responsibility consist in? The first question can be answered by saying that the notion of responsibility can legitimately be applied to one who has capacity of understanding, of reasoning, of imagining, of intending, of choosing, of deliberating, of willing and desiring etc., that is, human beings. Those who lack these capacities associated with responsibility, the concept of responsibility cannot be applied to them i.e., animals, insects, birds and material things or events. The second question can be answered by saying that one who has the capacities associated with responsibility is held responsible on the account of his free actions. The third question can be answered by saying that a person's responsibility consists in doing and owing what he himself or she herself chooses and assigns to himself or herself freely and consciously. This means that only a free conscious agent can be held to be responsible on the account of his action prescribed to himself or others, not to the actions and their results.

It is quite obvious from the above analysis that the notions of freedom and responsibility are opposed to fatalism and predestination but not to determinism. Freedom is opposed to fatalism because fatalism denies that human beings have the power to change the course of events[2], which the doctrine of freedom presupposes. In other words, according to fatalism, human being is impotent to do anything by himself. He cannot change the course of events by his own efforts and potential power. Whatever he does and exercises is all fated. He does not have any free will power either to cause or not to cause action, which the doctrine of freedom assumes. But fatalism cannot be accepted because the human beings are not mere victim of fate. They are conceived to have free will power either to cause or not to cause actions. Actions in this sense are within the control of their power. Before causing actions, human beings generally deliberate, choose, and plan actions for which they are morally held responsible and accountable for whatever they do. If everything is fated, and agents do not have power to change the course of events, they cannot be held responsible and accountable for whatever they do. The reason why the agents cannot be held responsible and accountable is that the notions of responsibility, accountability, and deserving are essentially associated with the notion of free action which fatalism denies. This we have already seen. Freedom and fatalism, thus, do not fall under the same logical category. Freedom contradicts fatalism and fatalism contradicts freedom. Unless we presuppose that the agents do have potential power to change the course of events through their actions, the notions of responsibility, accountability and deserving cannot legitimately be applied to them. We can neither condemn nor commend them on the basis of whatever they do, good or bad. Freedom is opposed to predestination because according to the theory of predestination, human beings do not have any freedom to choose, to decide, to plan or to do an action in which the freedom of action consists. The theory of predestination asserts that everything that happens is predestinated by God. God is the real cause of all actions. Human beings are mere instruments to carry out whatsoever are predestinated in them by God. If this view is correct, then it is not human beings but God, who should be held responsible for human actions, because He Himself is the originator of human actions and one who originates should be held responsible for whatever is originated which the doctrine of human freedom denies. Because according to the doctrine of human freedom, to be free is to determine and to determine is to be the authority of what is determined. In other words, freedom implies self-determinism and self-authority. A free human agent is one who himself chooses and originates his action. The source or the origin of action lies on him, not outside which the theory of predestination denies. Although human freedom is opposed to fatalism and predestination but it is not opposed to determinism, because determinism is the view that everything that happens is determined, which the doctrine of human freedom does not deny. The word 'determined' is an ambiguous word. It requires clarification. In everyday usage 'to be determined' is roughly taken in the sense of 'to be resolved'. But in the context of the problem of human freedom 'to be determined' is taken not in the sense of 'to be resolved', it is rather taken in the sense of 'to be caused'. When we take determinism in this sense, it does not contradict human freedom because it asserts that everything that happens has a cause. It does not say anything whether that cause is mental or physical; whether it is inorganic nature or organism or people or God. As far as the doctrine of determinism is concerned the cause can be anything. Determinism, in fact, is opposed to indeterminism but not freedom, because indeterminism denies what determinism asserts.

Although determinism is compatible with human freedom but it is not the ground of freedom. The doctrine of determinism is different from the doctrine of human freedom. The notion of determinism does not involve in it the absence of something i.e., constraints, compulsions etc. which the notion of freedom does. To say this does not amount to mean that freedom is unconnected with determinism. Freedom is not unconnected with determinism. In fact, human freedom is possible only on the assumption that determinism is true.[3] When an action is determined or caused by the agent himself freely and not caused by any other being or condition, we say that the agent is free and not otherwise. In distinguishing between free and unfree actions we do not try to mark the presence and absence of causes but attempt to indicate the kind of causes that are present.[4] We say an action is free when it is caused freely by the agent; otherwise it is called an unfree action. Both free and unfree actions are caused, but free actions are caused freely without any constraints while unfree actions are caused with the constraints. Thus what distinguishes free action from unfree action is not that one is caused and other is uncaused but the presence or the absence of certain conditions. Uncaused action is self-contradictory in terms. To make oneself free from or free to is not to make oneself free from actions. Human freedom does not consist in the renunciation of action or in inaction. It consists in action.

One might say that if everything that happens is determined (caused) by previously existing conditions and these in turn are caused by conditions prior to them and so on indefinitely back in time, human freedom becomes impossible, because human beings do not have control over the causes of actions which come prior to their existence. There is no doubt that human beings have no control over the causes which come prior to their existence. But to say this does not mean that determinism is incompatible with human freedom. The said problem arises due to the misunderstanding of the doctrine of determinism. The doctrine of determinism does not assert that whatever happens is caused by previously existing conditions and these in turn are caused by the conditions prior to them and so on indefinitely back in time. What it asserts is that everything that happens has a cause. And to say this is not to say that whatever causes is also caused by the antecedent conditions prior to it and so on indefinitely in time. When we confuse determinism with pre-ordination and fatalism only then the above mentioned problem arises; otherwise not. Free action involves determinism and is inconceivable without it. Determinism only says that whatever happens has some cause, and as long as that cause is the agent himself there is no restriction on the agent's freedom so far determinism is concerned. We do not become good or bad on the ground that we have been determined to be so by the forces outside of our control, as Hard determinists say.[5] We become good or bad by our deeds. No act is free unless its origin lies in the agent's free will. If an action is not caused by the agent's free will, it will not be his action and in that case we cannot assign responsibility and accountability of the action to him.

The upholders of the doctrine of *karma* classified *karmas* in two ways. First classification is done into *sancita, prārabdha* and *kriyamāna* (*āgāmi*).[6] While the second is done into *nitya, naimittika, kāmya* and *niṣiddha*.[7] The first classification is done basically between two classes: past *karma* and present *karma*. The past *karma* is further classified into *sancita* and *prārabdha.* In regard to *sancita* and *prārabdha karmas* there is no possibility of freedom. The possibility of freedom, if at all possible, is possible only in the context of *kriyamāna karma,* not in the context of *sancita* and *prārabdha.* Because *sancita* and *prārabdha karmas* are already done *karmas.* Actions which are already done, the question of making oneself free from certain conditions or to do certain things in regard to them does not arise at all. The question of freedom does arise in the context of action only when action is not done and there is a scope for its choosing and doing. Past actions being actions of the past fall outside of our control. But according to the doctrine of *karma,* we are bound to realize their fruits. And in realization of the fruits of *karma* of the past the agent is not free. He is bound to reap it. The difference between *sancita* and *prārabdha* consists merely in this fact that in the case of the former the fruits are yet to be realized while in the case of the latter the realization of the fruits have begun. Nonetheless, both the *karmas* are the stored *karmas* (*karma,* in fact, here is used not in the sense of action but in the sense of *karma phala* which is different from *karma* which causes it). The problem that arises in regard to the past *karma* does not arise in regard to *kriyamāna karma,* because *kriyamāna karma* is characterized as one which is yet to be done and what is yet to be done in regard to that there is a scope for the possibility of freedom. The agent can be said to have freedom either to choose or not to choose them. Not only this in cases where a series of action is continuing the agent can be conceived to have freedom either to stop them or to continue. Unless we presuppose freedom in the context of *kriyamāna karma,* we cannot talk of duties and responsibilities; nor can there be any scope for getting *mokṣa* from the bondage of *karma phala.* The second classification of *karma* is done into *nitya, naimittika, kāmya* and *niṣiddha. Nitya* and *naimittika* are obligatory actions. The actions that one is obliged to perform regularly are *nitya,* while those which are to be performed on the specific occasions are *naimittika,* those actions the performance of which is prohibited are called *niṣiddha karmas.* While deciding as to which actions are obligatory and which are prohibited, *Vedas* and *Smritis* are regarded as authorities. Actions which are done with some purpose or goal are called *kāmya karmas.* Nonetheless, whatever the *karma* may be, whether it is *nitya* or *naimittika;* whether it is *niṣiddha* or *kāmya,* it does not contradict human freedom. Obligatory and prohibited actions are not opposed to human freedom, because human beings do have freedom to choose or not to choose obligatory and prohibited actions prescribed by the *Vedas.* Actions become obligatory only when they are chosen. Non-chosen actions do not bind the individual to act upon them. The upholders of the doctrine of *karma* always presuppose human freedom of this kind. They do not say that the classification of *karma* into *nitya, naimittika, niṣiddha* and *kāmya* contradict human freedom.

Still one might argue that, human beings due to ignorance think and feel that they are free to choose between different alternative courses of action, while the fact is that they are not free at all, because which alternative human beings will choose in the context of *kriyamāna karma* had already been determined by his previous actions. And his previous actions are controlled by the previous of the previous actions and so on indefinitely back in time. *Karma* is beginningless. And if *karma* has a beginningless series then there is no scope for human freedom within the series of *karma.* The doctrine of *karma* rules out the very possibility of human freedom since human beings do not know all the antecedent conditions of the actions of the past, they do not feel bound or compelled. If they would have known in advance as to what they are going to decide at what time, the freedom of choice which they think they enjoy in choosing the alternative will cease to exist. Due to their ignorance they feel that they are free, actually they are not free at all. But this objection does not hold much matter. Because when we examine carefully, we find that it does not rule out the possibility of human freedom. The possibility of human freedom still exists. Because when it is said that *karma* is beginningless, it is said only in the sense that we do not know when did *karma* begin. And to say this is not to say that *karma* had no origin or beginning. All *karmas* do have origin, no matter whether their origins involve a reference to the past causes or to the present. But the origins of all actions ultimately lie in the agent. To say this does not mean that actions cannot be done in ignorance. It is perfectly quite possible that the agent may think that he is free and yet he may not be free because he may go wrong in his thinking. His thinking may be correct or incorrect. But saying this does not amount to contradicting the possibility of human freedom. Above all, the adherents of the doctrine of *karma* do not claim that the primal source of all actions lies outside the agent. What they say is that there are certain actions which are caused by the *karmas* of the past. And to say this is not to say that they totally eliminate the possibility of human freedom from the doctrine of *karma.* They do believe in the possibility of human freedom. In fact, the doctrine of *karma* becomes meaningful only on this presupposition that human beings do have power to make themselves free from certain conditions in order to do certain things. And it is on this presupposition the doctrine of *karma* holds human beings responsible and accountable for all that whatever happens in their life; otherwise the notion of responsibility in terms of accountability, which the *karmavādins* apply to them loose their meanings. Responsibility is not only essentially connected with the notion of free action but it is also essentially connected with the knowledge of action. Moral responsibility always presupposes the agent's free action and knowledge. After performing *karma* we have no control over its *karma phala. Karma phala* becomes inevitable according to the doctrine of *karma.* But before performing *karma,* the *karmavādins* do believe that we have power to control *karma* and its *phala* by not causing them. When a person is morally held responsible for his action, he is held responsible not on the basis of *karma phala* which his *karma* produces but on the basis of his *karma.* The ground of moral responsibility consists in the agent's free action. We cannot say in the same breath that we are free to choose certain actions at a particular time in a particular situation but we do not know that we are free unless we contradict. Moral responsibility is not connected with rightness or wrongness of an act with which reward and punishment are connected respectively. It is connected with the act itself. A person becomes responsible for the result of his *karma* because of his *karma,* not because of its rightness or wrongness. An occurrence over which we had no control is something we cannot be held responsible for. This means, in other words, that we can be held morally responsible only for those things which were/are within our control at a particular time and not that which were/are outside of our control at any time. Here one might ask this question : If an occurrence over which we had no control is something we cannot be held morally responsible for, then we should not be held responsible for *karma phala* because *karma phala* is an occurrence over which we had no control. If this be so, then what the doctrine of *karma* asserts is false. Because it asserts that man is responsible for the result of whatever he does, irrespective of whether it is done freely or unfreely. There is no doubt that in one sense, we can say that the agent has no control over the actual result of his action. He cannot predict in advance what kind of result his actions would be producing in future when it is done. And that is the reason why on the basis of the actual result of action he cannot be morally held responsible. But in another sense he can be held morally responsible for the result of his action because he had control over his action. Actions which were /are within his control to perform or not to perform do constitute the ground for holding him morally responsible and accountable for the results which are brought through them, no matter whether their results were intended or unintended, whether they involve a reference to the past or to the past of the past and so on. Actions which are yet to be done, that is, undone actions, not done actions, their results are within the agent's control. By controlling action (in the sense of not causing it) the agent can control the result of action which his action would have possibly produced, if he had done it. From this point of view, the agent could be held morally responsible for the result of his action. It is on this reason the doctrine of *karma* holds the agent responsible for the result of his action even if he had no control over the actual result of his action. Moreover, the *karmavādins* do not say that all the agent's present actions are the effects of his past actions and so on indefinitely in time. The problem does arise only when it is assumed that all human actions are controlled by his past actions and his past actions are controlled by the actions of the past of the past and so on indefinitely in time which the *karmavādins* do not assert. They do believe in the origin of *karma,* though they say that it is beginningless. Since they believe in the origin of *karma,* they also believe that there is an end of *karma.* This fact is quite obvious from the Indian conception of *mokṣa* itself. The Indian conception of the attainment of *mokṣa* strongly suggests that the agent can overcome his beginningless *karmas.* The notion of beginningless should not be taken in the sense of non-origination. It should be taken in the epistemic sense, that is, we do not know when it originated.

It is said[8] that in the Indian tradition freedom is incompatible with responsibility and the doctrine of *karma* because according to the Indian tradition, a person is supposed to be free when he attains the state of liberation *(mokṣa)* in terms of which freedom is defined. And when he attains the state of liberation, he has no responsibility to undertake in his life; he transcendents all the *karmas.* This means that on the account of the Indian tradition one cannot be both free and responsible at the same time. Either a person is responsible but not free, or he is free but not responsible. But this charge, to our mind, does not hold good to all the Indian traditions of thought. The concept of *mokṣa* has been analysed in different ways by the different schools of Indian philosophy. All the Indian schools of thought do share this view that *mokṣa* is a freedom from bondage and suffering of all sorts. But they do differ in other respects. According to some schools of thought (i.e., *Advaita Vedānta* and *Sāṁkhya*)[9], knowledge alone leads to *mokṣa* while according to some others [i.e., (*Jaina, Bauddha*)[10] and (*Viśiṣṭādvaita Vedānta*)[11]], both knowledge and right actions are required for the attainment of *mokṣa*. Difficulties crop up when we think that there is only one conception of freedom (*mokṣa*) in the Indian traditions of thought, which is not true. In the Indian traditions, the notion of freedom is used differently in the different contexts. When it is used in the context of disembodied self, it is understood in its absolute sense, but when it is used in the context of embodied self, i.e., human beings, it is not used in absolute sense. Even in the context of disembodied self the concept of freedom is not used in the same sense in the all Indian systems of thought. Nonetheless, freedom in both the cases do not mean one and the same thing. Freedom of the self does not mean freedom of will to act, to choose between actions or between action and inaction. Because the self, according to some Indian traditions (i.e., *Advaita Vedānta, Sāṁkhya)* , is not really subject to its will and action. When the self is called free (i.e., *mukta)* it is called in this sense that the self is not bound by any action, because it does not really do any action. So it is free from pleasure or pain also. From this point of view, we can say that the freedom of self is a freedom from certain conditions (i.e., ignorance and body) and not freedom to do certain actions in a particular situation at a particular time. While in the context of human beings and their actions, the concept of freedom is used not merely in the sense of 'freedom from' but a 'freedom to' as well. In the context of human actions, a freedom cannot be a freedom from if it is not also a freedom to. Because in the context of actions, to free oneself from something or other contextually implies to make oneself free to do something or other. If there were no need to act freely, there would neither be any need to free oneself from constraints. Since 'human freedom' is different from the 'freedom of self', to deduce one from the other would amount to committing a mistake. Indian conception of freedom (in the sense of *mokṣa*) becomes incompatible with responsibility and the doctrine of *karma* only when it is taken in the sense of freedom from the embodied self and the *karmas.* Because the question of responsibility does arise only in the context of action, in the domain of which the doctrine of *karma* has its validity. And the performance of action cannot be conceived without assuming the existence of body, because it is body through which actions are executed. In fact, the attainment of *mokṣa* , according to the Indian traditions of thought, is not possible without assuming human freedom. Above all, the Indian conception of *jīvanmukti* does not involve in it the renunciation of action and its correlated responsibility. It involves in it the renunciation of desire of getting the fruit of *karma* which strongly suggests that the Indian conception of freedom is not incompatible with responsibility and the doctrine of *karma,* at least in the context of *jīvanmukti.* Therefore it would be incorrect to pass this sweeping judgement that in the Indian traditions, freedom is incompatible with responsibility and the doctrine of *karma.* In fact, all the Indian traditions of thought presuppose human freedom which is compatible with responsibility and the doctrine of *karma.* This fact is quite obvious from their conception of *mokṣa* itself. The problem arises when we confuse the freedom of self with the freedom of human being. The freedom of self does not consist in free action, while the freedom of human being consists in free action, which implies the absence of certain conditions i.e., constraints, compulsions etc. But the source of the power of freedom in both the cases is linked with the metaphysical notion of self. The disembodied self is not bound by *karma* since it does not perform any sort of *karma,* while the embodied self is bounds by *karma.* But the embodied self is conceived not to be originally so. The human agential power which is associated with the metaphysical conception of self is a bound self (*jīva*), not an unbound self (*ātman*). The *jīva's* freedom is not incompatible with responsibility and the doctrine of *karma.* Though in all the Indian systems of thought ignorance is said to be the cause of bondage and *karma* (ignorance here is used in the metaphysical sense and not in the epistemic sense) but its removal is not denied, nor is it said that ignorance had no origin. What is said is that ignorance is beginningless, that is, we do not know when the human self (i.e., the bound self) got associated with ignorance. And to say this is not to say that the Indian conception of ignorance rules out the logical possibility of human freedom, in both the senses of the term i.e., the freedom of self and the freedom of human being. They are rather based on the presupposition of the doctrine of freedom.

Notes and References

1. John Hospers, *An Introduction to Philosophical Analysis*, Allied Publishers Private Ltd., 1971, p. 330.
2. *Ibid.*, 322.
3. *Ibid.*, p. 330.
4. Paul Edwards, *Hard and Soft Determinism*, quoted from *Determinism and Freedom in the age of Modern Science*, Edited by Sidney Hook, Collier Books, New York, 1961, p. 118.
5. Jacques. P. Thiroux, *Ethics Theory and Practice*, Glencoe Publishing Co. Inc., Encino, California, Collier MacMillan Publishers (London), 1977, p. 69.
6. K. K. Anand, *Indian Philosophy*, Bharatiya Vidya Prakashan, 1982, p. 314.
7. *Ibid.*, pp. 315-16.
8. A.B. Creel, *Dharma*, As An Ethical Category Relating to Freedom and Responsibility, *Philosophy East and West* (Vol. 22, No. 2, 1972), pp. 164-65.
9. K. K. Anand, *Indian Philosophy*, Bharatiya Vidya Prakashan, 1982, pp. 276-77.
10. *Ibid.*, pp. 277-78.
11. S. K. Maitra , *The Ethics of the Hindus*, University of Calcutta, 1956, p. 97.

5

Karma and Transmigration

The doctrine of *karma* states a conjunction of the following things : (i) Every action produces some result which may be either pleasurable or painful no matter whether it is moral or immoral, *Vedic* or non-*Vedic*, religious or non-religious, good or bad. It not only asserts that every action produces some result, but also asserts that every action produces its fitting result, that is, good action produces good result and bad action produces bad result and no good action produces bad result or bad action produces good result in any condition. (ii) The doer of action necessarily experiences or realises the result of his/her action in the present or next life. (iii) The doer of action deserves the result of action because of his/her action.

(i) and (ii) make a factual claim, but (iii) makes a moral claim, as it says that the doer deserves or ought to have some experiences because of his/her action done in the past or present life. (ii) and (iii) conjointly assert that every doer necessarily or inevitably gets what he deserves and does not get what he does not deserve which means that there is no undeserved or unjustified happiness or suffering in the world of agent. (ii) Asserts that whatever agent's action entitles him to get, he is bound to get; if he does not get in this life, he will surely get in the next life. If he has got something for which no action done by him in the present life is responsible, it would amount to mean that some action done by him in his previous life is responsible. (ii) and (iii) make it quite obvious that retributive notion of justice is built in the conception of the doctrine of *karma*. The conjunction of (i), (ii) and (iii) indicate that *karma* causes bondage, in the sense that because of *karma* the agent is inextricably caught up in the cycle of the *karmic* bondage. (i) and (ii) conjuncts indicate a descriptive, factual or empirical characteristics of the doctrine of *karma*. While (iii) conjunct indicates its moral or ethical characteristic. Indian thinkers have interpreted the doctrine of *karma* in both the ways, factual and ethical, on the grounds of the assertions of (i), (ii) and (iii) conjuncts. (i), (ii) and (iii) conjuncts not only indicate that actions cause bondage but also indicate the monistic and self-centric characteristics of the doctrine of *karma*. Because they conjointly attribute everything good or bad, one has or will ever have to only one kind of causes i.e., to his and only his actions which is neither provable nor refutable by any evidence obtained from experiences. When Hiriyanna says, "...it traces all suffering to ourselves and thus removes bitterness against god or our neighbour,"[1] he says it only on the basis of the monistic characteristic of the doctrine of *karma*. A conjunction of (i), (ii) and (iii) not only involves monistic and retributive elements of justice in it, but also a fatalistic element in the sense that the agent has no power to change the course of *karmic* experiences resulting from his good and bad *karmas* of the past or the present life.

But to believe in the assertion of (ii) that one is bound to get the result of his/her action, means believing in the theory of (iv) transmigration of soul and (v) *karmic* residues since the latter is built in the belief of the former. If the agent is bound to get what his actions entitled him to and if one does not get all that he is entitled to in the present life, then there must be a life after death to enable him to get the unrealized balance. Likewise, if agent has got something for which no action done by him in the present life is responsible then he must have had a previous life, actions done in which are responsible for his unaccounted *karmic* experiences. But to believe in (iv), that is, in the transmigration of soul means believing in the substantivity and permanency of the soul. Because the latter is built in the belief of the former. The transmigration of soul from one life to another life is not possible without assuming the permanency of the soul. This follows from the meaning of the notion of transmigration of soul itself. There can be no migration of soul from one life to another life or from one body to another body unless we assume that the soul exists and persists at different times. The term 'migration of soul' implies persistence and continuity i.e., the existence of one and the same soul at different times. So to believe in the theory of rebirth means believing in the identity and permanency of the substantial self. But the belief in the transmigration of soul neither entails nor is entailed by the belief in the transmigration of *karmic* residues. Both the beliefs are different but are intertwined. To believe in the transmigration of *karmic* residues (or *saṁskāras*) means to believe in the principle of conservation of *saṁskāras*, that is, *saṁskāras* do not perish before the realization of their consequences and persist and exist at different times. To believe in (iv) and (v) means to believe in the theory of *saṁsāra* or the continued existence of the self with *karmic* residues in a succession of lives since the latter is built in the beliefs of (iv) and (v). This implies that birth is not the beginning of the existential identity of the particular *jīva* and death is not the cessation of its existential status. The identity of the phenomenal self (*jīva*) persists through different life times. The existence of the *jīva* is not terminated at the end of death, but is transformed and continues to exist and is "reborn" (reincarnation, trans-incarnation).

It is evident from the conjunction of (i), (ii), (iii), (iv) and (v) that the notions of *karma, saṁsāra* and transmigration are conceptually connected. This has been made explicit by M. Hiriyanna :

> "Since, however, those causes cannot all be found within the narrow limits of a single life, it postulates the theory of *saṁsāra* or the continued existence of the self (*jīva*) in a succession of lives. Thus the theory of transmigration is a necessary corollary to the doctrine of *karma*."[2]

Like Hiriyanna, Deutsch also acknowledges their conceptual connection in his book *Advaita Vedānta,*

> "...when the term '*karma*' is used it refers to the joint doctrine of the 'law' of *karma*—the principle of causality which holds that all moral actions produce moral effects—and of *saṁsāra*—the principle that there is a transmigration of the self (the *sūkṣmaśarīra*) or 'subtle body' in a series of births, deaths and rebirths."[3]

The belief in the doctrine of *karma* is meaningless unless we believe in the transmigration of soul and ontology of the *karmic* residues. Transmigration of soul and *karmic* residues constitute as a necessary corollary to the *karma*-doctrine. Rebirth is meaningless without *karma* and *karma* is not possible without birth. If we believe that the soul is repeatedly reborn in the body, we must also believe that there is some link between the lives that preceded and the lives that follow. The classical Indian thinkers believe that the *karma* provides link between the lives of the past, present and future. But none of these *karmic* beliefs including belief in the transmigration of soul and the existence of *karmic* residues can be established or validated on the empirical grounds. The *karmic* beliefs are of such kind that they are neither provable nor refutable by means of any evidence obtained from sensuous experiences, nor can we say that transmigration is scientifically possible. Because, the scientific procedure of observation, quantification, mensuration and controlled experimentation do not have any applicability in the realm of *karma.* The *karmic* beliefs are mere dogmatic beliefs. One who does not believe in the transmigration of soul or rebirth would hesitate to accept the intelligibility of the doctrine of *karma.*

When we go into the logical analysis of the theory of transmigration, we find that transmigration without *karma* is not possible according to the *karmavādins.* Because in their view it is the *karma* which makes transmigration possible, no matter whether it is transmigration of *saṁskāras* or soul or both. Transmigration of *karma phala* from one life to another life presupposes the ontological existence of *karma phala* and the ontological existence of *karma phala* cannot be conceived apart from and independent of *karma* and *kartā* in the sense that without *kartā* no *karma* is possible and without *karma* no *karma phala* is conceivable. This means that transmigration of *karma phala* in the form of *saṁskāras* is essentially linked with *karma* and *kartā* in the agent-cause paradigm of *karma*. The transmigration of soul from one body to another body is not possible in view of the *karmavādins* (those who believe in the transmigration of self) without the admissibility of the existence of *karma phala,* because what makes soul to move from one body to another body or from one life to another life is the force of the *karma phala* which soul possesses. This means that the force which makes transmigration possible consists in the efficacious power of *karma* and *karma phala,* and not in anything else. In other words, in the *karmic* theory it is the *karma-bīja* (act force) which is responsible for the transmigration of soul and *karmic saṁskāras*. If there were no *karma*, there would not be any act-force; and consequently there would not be any rebirth or the reincarnation of soul. The act-force is a link that connects the past, present and future lives of man. This has been accepted in Hinduism, Buddhism and Jainism. If it is the act-force which makes transmigration possible, it logically comes prior to the process of transmigration and not vice-versa. From this point of view, we can say that *karma* is a postulate of the doctrine of transmigration of soul and *saṁskāras*. But if we go by the *karmic* assertion of (ii), the belief in the transmigration of soul and *saṁskāras* is built in the *karmic* assertion itself without assuming of which the assertion of (ii) does not make any sense. The belief in the transmigration of soul and *saṁskāras* do constitute as a part of the meaning of the *karmic* assertion. The act-force is different from the force of self. By the 'act-force' we mean the causal efficacy of the act. The causal efficacy of the act consists in the producing of some result which lies in the act itself and that is quite different from the force of self. The force of self lies in the self itself. It is not derived from the act-force. It rather makes the act possible. From this point of view, we can say that the force of self is a metaphysical postulate of the ontological existence of act. Although the force of self is a metaphysical postulate of the ontological existence of the act-force but it by itself does not make the act-force possible. The ontological existence of the act-force assumes the unity of body and soul. Without body and bodily muscle contraction no act is possible. To say this does not mean that the phenomena of action can be understood and explained in terms of physical events alone, without making any reference to the existence of a conscious entity. This we have already seen in Chapter II. Because of this reason we have said that it is the embodied self i.e., the human being who performs action, and not the soul or the body. The theory of transmigration presupposes the theory of act-force and the theory of act-force presupposes the unity of self and body and the unity of self and body cannot be explained in terms of the forces of act since it comes logically prior to them. Perhaps it is because of this reason the *karmavādins* introduced the idea of ignorance as primal cause to explain the unity of soul and body. The belief in the primal ignorance itself requires investigation in which we shall not enter in the present context. One who does not believe in the existence of self and its force would hesitate to accept the doctrine of transmigration of self and rebirth.

But one who believes in the doctrine of transmigration of soul is bound to believe in *saṁsāra*. *Saṁsāra* is a sanskrit word. It is derived from the root *sṛ* which means 'to flow', 'run swiftly', or 'glide', conjoined with the prefix *saṁ*, meaning 'with' or 'together'. The word has the original sense of a flowing with or together.[4] Those who translate the word '*saṁsāra*' as 'transmigration', 'reincarnation', 'metempsychosis', 'rebirth' and 'the round of birth and death', for them *saṁsāra* is a beginningless or ever-recurring series of births and deaths. It is bondage(*bandha*) to the embodied life in spatio-temporal world. It is imprisonment of the eternal spirit in a destructible impure body. For them rebirth, transmigration and *saṁsāra* are synonymous terms. But when we go into the analysis of the notion of *saṁsāra*, we find that it is different from the notions of transmigration and rebirth. The notions of transmigration and rebirth are conceptually linked with the notion of *saṁsāra* in the sense that without perpetual existence transmigration and rebirth are not possible. But the notion of *saṁsāra* is not conceptually linked with the notions of transmigration of soul and rebirth. The notion of *saṁsāra* involves in its meaning the notion of ceaseless flow or change or succession or series. And from this point of view, we can say that *saṁsāra* is the state of constant flow or flux. It does not necessarily involve in its meaning the substantial and essential identity of a thing which can be said remains unchanged in the process of flow or change. What constitutes the meaning of *saṁsāra* is a ceaseless process or change or continuity, which does not by itself involve in its meaning the notions of identity, persistence, permanency and stability of a thing of the *saṁsāra*. This implies that the notion of *saṁsāra* is conceptually and essentially linked with the notions of succession, change, flow or gliding but not with the notions of identity, stability, permanency and persistency of a thing with which the notions of transmigration of soul, *karma*, reincarnation and rebirth are essentially connected. The notion of *saṁsāra* is based on the theory of flow or change and the notion of flow or change involves in it a reference to preceding and succeeding events and it goes on continuing without involving the notion of eternity or identity of anything. In the flow the preceding and the succeeding events are conceived to have the ontological existence because of their capacity of producing the succeeding events. This implies that one who believes in *saṁsāra* is not necessarily bound to believe in the identity of a thing belonging to the *saṁsāra*. But the notions of transmigration of soul and *karmic* residues are linked with the notions of identity, permanency, persistency and stability of a thing in some way or the other. The transmigration of soul with the *karmic* residues assumes the identity of actor and action in the continuity of the series of life. It is the identity of *kartā-bhoktā-karma phala* that makes the theory of rebirth or transmigration or reincarnation meaningful and intelligible. To deny this would amount to mean the denial of responsibility in the sense of accountability and deserving which the agent owes and earns on the account of his deeds. Ethical responsibility assumes the continuity of the ethical agent and the continuity of the ethical agent assumes the identity, permanency, stability and persistency of the agent and the *karma phala* of his *karma* in some sense or the other. Negation of the latter implies the negation of the former. It does not matter whether we assign the same amount of permanency, stability and persistency to the actor and the *karmic* residues of his action and their unity or not. What matters is that unless we assume some amount of stability, permanency and persistency of the agent and the *karmic* residues, neither the notion of identity of the agent nor the notions of rebirth and *karma phala* make any sense. Not only this, the doctrine of *karma* also would fail to explain the *karmic* phenomena of the *jīva* or the agent for which it was designed. It would loose its explanatory power.

From the above discussions it is quite evident that the notions of *karma, saṁsāra* and transmigration are different and distinct and yet they are conceptually and essentially connected. Transmigration is not possible without believing in *saṁsāra* because it is the *karmic saṁsāra* in which the transmigration of phenomenal *jīva* takes place. And what makes the transmigration of phenomenal *jīva* possible is the force of his act. The notion of transmigration of self including *karma phala* does not preclude the notion of identity in continuity of the series of life. But the notion of continuity or flow with which the notion of *saṁsāra* is essentially linked precludes the notion of identity. But to say this does not amount to mean that the notion of identity is incompatible with the notion of *saṁsāra*. Both the notions are quite compatible since the acceptance of one does not necessarily imply the rejection of the other. The identity of agent is possible to conceive through the changes of his characteristics acquired by his deeds, good or bad. The concept of the identity of the *karmic* agent assumes the possibility of identifying of that agent when referred to under different descriptions. From this point of view, we can say that the notion of identifying involves in it the notion of 'something is the same', that is, the existence of one and the same thing at different times. The problem of inconsistency that arises in regard to the notions of identity and *saṁsāra* arises because of not understanding the scope of the predication involves in the phrase 'one and the same'. The identity predicates are attributed to the agent and his *karma phala;* and to attribute the identity predicates to the agent and his *karma phala* does not amount to mean that the agent cannot acquire new *karmic* characteristics through his deeds, nor does it mean that he cannot leave the acquired *karmic* characteristics of the past or the present deeds. The notion of identity implies persistence, that is, the existence of one and the same thing at different times and that is quite possible with the admissibility of change in the sense that the agent may acquire different descriptions through his deeds. If he is bad, he can be good, and if he is good, he can be bad. To maintain the theory of identity of the agent does not amount to mean that the agent cannot acquire or leave certain contingent characteristics. At different times in the continuous series of lives the agent can acquire different *karmic* characteristics and these characteristics in turn contingently may constitute the criterion of the identity of the agent in the continuous process of the change. Since it is possible for the agent to possess the different *karmic* characteristics at different times without losing his identity in the sense of his essence, he can have different forms in the *karmic* world. Not only this, it is also possible for him to be reborn in the different species on the account of his *karma phala,* and this does not contradict the identity of the agent in the explained sense of the term. So it is possible for a human being to be reborn in the form of some other creature. And the new form of the other creature is his extrinsic form and his extrinsic form does not contradict his inner intrinsic identity. Acquired forms and characteristics keep on coming and going in the life series of the agent, but his soul is believed persists throughout the changes of lives in its essence. Unless we assume it, the belief in *karma* and transmigration of soul does not make any sense. The *karmic* agent has to be assumed, as the embodiment of both essential and accidental characteristics. Then and then alone we can meaningfully talk of the continuing identity of the agent in the *karmic* phenomenal world. In the paradigm of *karma* the notion of *saṁsāra* is used in a technical sense and not in the sense of a universe or a world, as it is generally understood. When we talk of personal identity in the world of *karma,* our talk always involves a reference either to the agent (self) or his *karmic* residues or both. And therefore the criterion of personal identity has to be examined only in the connection with the agent and his *karma.* Bodily features, which constitute the criterion of identity in ordinary life, do not constitute the criterion of identity of the agent in the *karmic* world. Different *karmas* lead to the possession of different forms of body. How it takes place about this different systems of Indian philosophy have different views. But it does take place in the view of the *karmavādins* of different systems, which cannot be ascertained whether it is true or false on the basis of the evidences of sensuous experiences. Because this belief is of such kind that it does not fall within the jurisdiction of our sensuous scientific experiences and methods.

Although all the Indian systems of thought except Cārvāka believe in the theory of *karma,* transmigration and the ontological existence of *saṁsāra,* but they disagree as regard to what it is that transmigrates and how it takes place. The Cārvāka school does not believe in the theory of the transmigration of soul including *karmic* residues because according to this school, everything, human and non-human, in this world is constituted and made up of the four *mahābhūtas* (elements) i.e., *pṛthivī* (earth), *ap* (water), *tejas* (fire) and *vāyu* (air). All the living things are different manifestations of the same pattern of mechanical combinations of these simple constitutive elements alone. Consciousness, body, senses and objects are nothing but the results of the different combinations of elements. Since the Cārvākas reduce self to the different combinations of elements, they explain the phenomena of actions merely in terms of physical elements without believing in the permanent self and its transmigration from life to life along with the *karmic* residues, which is believed to be possessed by the self through actions. Unlike Cārvāka, Sāṁkhya believes that self (*puruṣa*) is different from *prakṛti.* It is the *prakṛti* which performs action but not the *puruṣa.* According to this school, the *puruṣa* is inactive and hence cannot perform by its nature any sorts of action, no matter whether it is good or bad or indifferent. Sāṁkhya explains the phenomena of actions in terms of the functions of the *guṇas* of *prakṛti.* According to this view, the *puruṣa* as such is neither bound, nor is it liberated, nor does it transmigrate. Bondage, liberation and transmigration belong to the *prakṛti* in its manifold forms, "*tasmān na badhyatéddhā na muchyate nāpi saṁsarati kashchid. saṁsarati badhyate muchyate cha nānāshrayā prakṛtiḥ*."[5] From the transcendental point of view, Sāṁkhya does not believe in the transmigration of self (*puruṣa*), but from the phenomenal point of view, it does believe in the transmigration of the bound self and the *karmic* residues. On his account, the phenomenal self undergoes birth and death and differs in qualities according to the deeds. In fact, the phenomenal self, on the account of Sāṁkhya system, is nothing but the ego which transmigrates along with the *karmic* residues acquired from one birth to another birth and the ego is one of the evolutes of *prakṛti*. Thus transmigration and *karma* belong to the non-self, that is, the *prakṛti* and not to the *puruṣa* And this view of Sāṁkhya is inconsistent with the theory of *karma*. Because according to the theory of *karma*, it is the agent, a conscious entity, not the *prakṛti* nor even its any one of the evolutes which is believed to be migrating from one life to another life in the world of *karma*. The theory of *karma*, as we have already pointed out, does assume not only the transmigration of *karmic* residues but also the transmigration of self which possesses the *karmic* residues and this Sāṁkhya denies, which is inconsistent with the *karmic* beliefs. Like Sāṁkhya, Advaita Vedānta also does not believe in the transmigration of self in the real sense. According to this system, it is due to ignorance we believe that the self is subject to the cycle of birth, death and rebirth. While Jainism and Nyāya-Vaiśeṣika believes in the real transmigration of self and *karmic* residues despite of their differences about the nature of self and the *karmic* residues. According to Jainism, the *jīva* (self) transmigrates through different domains of the entire living world. *Jīvas* differ in both quality and quantity. Unlike Jainism, Nyāya-Vaiśeṣikas believes that consciousness is an accidental characteristic of the self. But they hold like Jainism that human beings and other organisms have the same self in essence, prone to transmigration and subject to the law of *karma*.[6] Like Nyāya-Vaiśeṣika, Mīmāṁsakas also believes that human and non-human beings have the same self which transmigrates in the entire domain of the living world in spite of their differences as regard to the nature of the self and the *karmic* residues. Jainism, Sāṁkhya, Nyāya-Vaiśeṣika, Mīmāṁsakas and Vedānta share this view that the agent who performs actions cannot be understood and explained purely in terms of psycho-physical events as Buddhism advocates. Buddhism does not believe in the transmigration of soul, but it does believe in the transmigration of *karma* in the form of *saṁskāra* s. According to this school, transmigration of *karmic* residues is possible without the transmigration of self from birth to birth For the Buddhist, soul is nothing but a bundle of the five *skandhas-rūpa* (matter), *vedanā* (feeling), *saṁjñā* (perception), *saṁskāra* (disposition) and *vijñāna* (consciousness). Unlike the other classical Indian systems of thought, Buddhism does not believe in the identity of *kartā* and *bhoktā*, nor does it presuppose the metaphysical notion of *kartā* to explain the phenomena of actions. The Buddhists explain actions merely in terms of psycho-physical events without assuming any permanent self which is claimed to be experiencing the result of *karmas*, good or bad, from one life to another life. The notion of identity, in their view, is a false notion . There is no soul which can be said to be migrating from one life to another life to reap the results of *karmas*. What transmigrates from one life to another life according to the Buddhists is *karma* and nothing else. The Buddhist's conception of self comes closer to Hume's conception of self. Like Buddhism, Hume also does not believe in the permanent self. For him,

> "when I enter most intimately into what I call *myself*, I always stumble on some particular perception or others, of heat or cold, light or shade, love or hatred, pain or pleasure. I never can catch *myself* at any time without a perception , and never can observe anything but the perception ."[7]

Like Heraclitus, Hume, William James, the Buddhism denies eternalism, essentialism and substantialism and negates the existence of permanent self which the doctrine of *karma* assumes, as we have seen in our analysis. Buddhism believes in the doctrines of impermanency (*anityatā*), momentariness (*kṣaṇabhaṅgavāda*) and non-soul (*anātmavāda*). Since the Buddhists believe in the thesis that everything in the universe of anthropocentric as well as non-anthropocentric is necessarily subject to production, destruction, change and impermanency, no matter whether it is a thing or organism or agent or action or the result of action, they deny the transmigration of permanent self but not *karma* which is inconsistent with their metaphysical doctrines. If everything is perishable and subject to production, destruction and change, the Buddhists cannot hold consistently this view with their theory of transmigration of *karma*. The *karma* is also liable to destruction and change and hence cannot be said to be migrating from one life to another life as the Buddhists say. In other words, the Buddhists cannot maintain consistently the thesis that *karma* transmigrates from life to life with their metaphysical doctrines. If the notion of identity is illusion, the notion of *karmic* identity is also illusion; and if the notion of *karmic* identity is illusion, it makes no sense to say, as they say, that the *karma* without an agent migrates from life to life. The question of *karmic* identity and its transmigration without assuming some amount of stability and permanency of the *karma phala* is not possible because the concept of identity, no matter whether we talk about it in the context of self or *karma* , implies persistence, that is, the existence of one and the same thing at different times which the Buddhists deny. The Buddhists belief in the transmigration of *karma* is inconsistent with their doctrines of impermanency and momentariness. No doubt one may conceive the transmigration of *karmic* residues from one life to another life, without assuming of any transmigrating soul. But the *karmic* ethical phenomena cannot be explained without assuming the existence of permanent self because ethical notions like the notions of responsibility, accountability, deserving and experiencing the fruit of *karma* in the present or in the next life always involve a reference to a permanent conscious agent, without assuming of which the *karmic* ethical notions cannot be understood, nor do they make any sense. If there is no agent persisting through different periods of time, we can neither identify him nor his actions and their results. There would be no one to take the moral responsibility of action. The fallacies of *kṛtapraṇāśa* and *akṛtābhyāgama* are logically bound to occur. An ethical *karmic* system which suffers from the fallacies of kṛtapraṇāś*a* and *akṛtābhyāgama* cannot explain satisfactorily whatsoever happens in the human and non-human life which an ethical *karmic* system is supposed to explain.

One might say that without assuming any identifiable self it is possible to explain moral responsibility following the framework of the Buddhists ethics. Because Buddhism believes that there is a continuity in the *karmic* process, the successive elements in the *karmic* process belong to the same *karmic* energy and that is enough to explain the ethical notion of responsibility. Moral responsibility is transferred from one element to another and the *karmic* potentiality belongs to no one else but the successive elements in the stream of life. And this shows that the Buddhists theory of transmigration of *karma* does not deny moral responsibility of the human being. There is no doubt that Buddhism believes that there is a continuity in the *karmic* process and in the *karmic* process the preceding element causally produces the succeeding element and the capacity to produce an effect proves its existence. But this is not enough to explain moral responsibility in terms of accountability because the notion of responsibility involves in its meaning the notion of agency and the notion of agency, cannot be explained merely in terms of preceding and succeeding events. The notion of moral responsibility does make sense only when we assume that in the continuity of the *karmic* process there exists a permanent conscious being, who not only performs *karma* but also takes the responsibility associated with it, which the Buddhistic *karmic* system denies.

The objection may be put forward by saying that if it is one and the same self which exists and persists in the *karmic* process throughout from one life to another life, then how can we say that it takes birth and rebirth ? The notion of birth and rebirth cannot legitimately be applied to the permanent eternal self. The answer to this question is : In the paradigm of *karma* the notions of birth, death and rebirth have been used in the technical senses and not in the ordinary senses. Birth is understood in the sense of association of the self with the body and death is understood in the sense of dissociation of the self from the body. Rebirth is understood in the sense of association of the self with the new body after death. Birth and death are mere stages and events in the ongoing continuous history of a given person. Birth is not the beginning of the existential identity of the particular person and death is not the cessation of his existential status. In the cycle of *karma*, birth, death and rebirth are different stages and are linked with one another. In the cycle of *karma,* birth could be said to be the beginning of death and death could be said to be the beginning of birth from different angles. Birth, death and rebirth, hence are relative terms. They are conceptually and ontologically connected with one another in the paradigm of *karma.* When the *karmavādins* talk about the rebirth of the soul, they use the word 'rebirth' in the sense of association of the self with new body after death. They do not mean that it is the soul (self) which is subject to birth, death and rebirth. Those who believe in the theory of the transmigration of soul maintain that the soul in its essence is neither born nor does it die, because to become existent from not being is called birth and to become non-existent from being is called death. The soul is devoid of either of these conditions. This means the soul is devoid of birth and death and does not decrease or increase; it is never destroyed even if the body is destroyed.[8] The soul is indestructible (*avināshi*), eternal (*nitya*), unborn (*aja*), immortal (*ajar*) and everlasting (*śāśvata*). It does not perish along with the body after death, nor is it born with body. On their account, it is the individual's body which is subject to birth and death. Just as a person casts off worn-out garments and puts on the new ones, so does the soul cast off worn-out bodies and enters into others that are new.[9] Further, when the *karmavādins* talk about the identity of self and the personal identity, they do not use them in the same sense, nor do they restrict the use of identity to the present life only. They extend its use to life after death, that is, the future life. The identity of self, on their view, consists in its persistency throughout the cycle of birth, death and rebirth. When the *karmavādins* talk about the personal identity, they talk it in the respect of the identity of embodied self (i.e., *jīva*) which is quite different from the identity of body. The identity of body is not the criterion of the identity of self, nor is it the sole criterion of the identity of *jīva* in the context of the transmigration of soul. The identity of *jīva* consists in the identity of self and the *karmic* residues besides the identity of body.

The *karmavādins* those who believe in the transmigration of soul also believe in the transferability of *karmic* residues from one life to another life so far as the life of a particular person is concerned that is agent, but deny by and large its transferability from the life of one person to another person. In other words, the *karmavādins* believe that the *karmic* residues pass from one life to another life of a person but they do not believe that the *karmic* residues pass from one individual's life to another individual's life which can be entitled as genetic *karmas*. Those who believe in it, their accounts suffer from the fallacies of *kṛtapraṇāśa* and *akṛtābhyāgama* and fail to provide justification for all that happens in the individual's life. The *Upaniṣads*[10] and the *Manusmriti*[11] no doubt believe in the transferability of *karmic* residues from one individual's life to another, but their account of the genetic *karma*, to our mind, does not seem to be ethically tenable thesis in the paradigm of *karma*. Those who believe in the theory of *karma*, quite often defend the transferability of soul and *karma*, on the basis of the evidences of memory of the past life. How far this view is correct is no doubt a matter of investigation.

Why the transferability of *karmic* residues from one individual's life to another individual's life is not possible is a relevant question which the *karmavādins* seem to have not answered. The thesis of non-transferability of the *karmic* residues from one individual's life to another individual's life, if at all possible, can be said to be possible only when we assume the inseparability of the individual's *karmic* residues with his soul or self. Not only this, we have to further assume the plurality of souls, then and then alone the thesis of non-transferability of *karma* from one individual's life to another can be maintained consistently. But all the *karmavādins* do not believe in the plurality of souls. Those who do not believe in the plurality of soul (self) in their context the question of the transferability of *karmic* residues does not arise at all. It arises only when we believe in the plurality of the lives on the basis of the plurality of self. Although all the *karmavādins* differ from one another as regard to the question of the transferability of *karmic* residues but they do believe in the ultimate separability of self and *karmic* residues and that is quite obvious from their belief in *mokṣa*.

All the classical Indian schools of thought except Cārvāka believe that freedom from the cycle of birth, death and rebirth is possible. But how it is possible and what makes it possible, on these questions they have different opinions. Despite that they all believe that ignorance as the primal cause of *karmic* bondage. Some Indian schools of thought, like Sāṁkhya and Vedānta, maintain that freedom from the *karmic* bondage or the cycle of birth, death and rebirth is possible through knowledge and knowledge alone. In their view, all the *karmas* are binding, no matter whether they are good or bad, moral or immoral, religious or non-religious, attached or detached. Moral and religious actions, on their account, no doubt purify mind which is required for the attainment of liberation but are not essential for the attainment of *mokṣa*. In fact, in their view, the notions of bondage and liberation do have meanings only in the world or phenomena, not in the world of self. Because the self, according to them, is not subject to bondage and liberation. It is due to ignorance, they say, we believe that we are in bondage and get liberation from it. Whereas the fact, according to them, is that the individual self from the transcendental point of view is beyond bondage and liberation, because it does not perform any action as such. The self never acts nor is it ever acted upon, therefore the question of its *karmic* bondage and liberation from it does not arise.

But this account of self is incompatible with the doctrine of *karma*. Those who believe in the Sāṁkhya and Advaitin's conception of self cannot maintain consistently it with the doctrine of *karma*. Because the doctrine of *karma*, as we have already seen, essentially assumes the agency of self and not the non-agency of self in which the schools of Sāṁkhya and Vedānta believe.

But some classical Indian schools of thought like Jainism, Buddhism, Mīmāṁsa and Viśiṣṭādvaita believe, unlike Sāṁkhya and Vedānta, that freedom from the chain of birth, death and rebirth is not possible through knowledge and knowledge alone. According to them, besides knowledge right action is also essentially required. But their opinions differ as regard to which one is more important or primary. Some of them give more importance to right knowledge, while the others give more importance to right action. Those who assign more importance to right action believe that right knowledge dawns when right actions are performed. But those who assign more importance to right knowledge believe that right action is not possible without right knowledge. However, it does not matter whether right knowledge is more important or right action. What is considered to be important is that right knowledge and right action both are essentially required in their opinion to obtain freedom from the cycle of rebirth. Although all these schools of thought agree on this point that right knowledge and right action are essentially required to obtain freedom from the *karmic* bondage but their opinions differ again as regard to the acquisition of right knowledge and right action. However, in spite of this they all believe that the acquisition of right knowledge makes the *sancita* (i.e, actions which were done in the previous life but have not yet begun to fructify) and non-attached *sancıyamāna* (i.e., actions which are being done in the present life) actions ineffective by destroying their causal potency. Thus, on their account, when the *prārabdha* (i.e., actions which were done in the previous life and whose residues have started fructifying) *karmas* exhaust their effects, the person who acts with right knowledge and non-attachment exhausts all his *karmic* liabilities which bind him with the chain of rebirth and makes himself free from bondage.

But when we critically reflect on both the accounts of the classical Indian systems of thought, we find that their accounts are based on this assumption that ignorance and attachment cause the bondage. Between these two causes, ignorance is considered to be the basic and real cause of birth, death and rebirth. Since they consider ignorance as the basic cause of bondage (in both epistemic and ontic senses) and ignorance can be removed only by knowledge alone, they advocate the thesis that freedom from bondage cannot be obtained without knowledge. But when we ask the question : How did the free self get associated with ignorance in the beginning before the unity of self and body which is pure consciousness in its essence, we do not find any satisfactory answer to it. If ignorance is said is inseparably connected with the self, the liberation of the self from ignorance is impossible; and if ignorance is external to the self, it cannot bind the self which is pure consciousness in its nature. All the *karmavādins* believe that the relation of ignorance and self is beginningless (in both epistemic and ontic senses) but do not believe that their association is inseparable. They all believe that ignorance is separable from the self through knowledge. But the question is : If the pure self can get infected by ignorance before the bondage, then there is no guarantee that it cannot again get infected by ignorance after liberation. If the soul can be tinged with ignorance before bondage, it can also be tinged with ignorance after liberation. If this be the case, complete liberation does not make any sense in which the *karmavādins* believe. A liberated soul can become bound and a bound soul can become liberated. Further, those who believe that non-attachment is a necessary condition to obtain freedom from bondage think that the acquisition of right knowledge is possible through the means of the renunciation of desire and not the renunciation of action. In their view, when actions are performed in detached spirit, they do not bind the individuals. But when the question is asked : How the renunciation of desire in action is possible ? The answer is given that it is possible through the acquisition of right knowledge, which they assume is possible only through the means of non-attachment, from which it is quite obvious that they do not hold a consistent view. If desire causes bondage, it causes bondage no matter what it is, whether it is a desire for getting the consequences of action or it is a desire for getting liberation. If desire as such is binding, it binds in all its cases no matter what they are. But all the *karmavādins* do not believe in it. They believe that all desires attached to the consequence of action and not action are binding except the desire for *mokṣa,* which they cannot hold consistently along with their thesis that desired acts as binding force. When the question is asked: Why does a desireful action bind and not desireless ? We do not find any satisfactory answer to it. If all actions originate from desire and it is desire which leads the individual to perform actions; a desireless action becomes impossible. And if a desireless action is possible, then it is incorrect to say that all actions originate from desire in which the *karmavādins* believe. Desire surely cannot be said to be the cause of the unity of soul and body, since it arises from their unity. All the desire elements belong to the domain of body and not to the domain of self and hence cannot provide as a postulate to understand and explain the unity of soul and body which is considered as a cause of bondage. The *karmavādins* do not seem to hold a consistent thesis on the causes of bondage. Sometimes they say, it is desire that causes bondage. And sometimes they say, it is action that causes bondage. Sometimes they say, it is not the action that causes bondage but desire for getting the result of action that causes bondage. If it is the action that causes bondage, it causes bondage no matter what it is, whether it is good action or bad action; whether it is *Vedic* action or non-*Vedic* action; whether it is moral action or non-moral action; whether it is done in attached manner or detached manner. If it is the desire for getting the consequences of action that causes bondage, it causes bondage even before performing the actual action, since it comes logically prior to it. If this be the case, no matter whether we cause or do not cause action, we become bound just by having some desire for getting something, which does not seem to be a sound thesis along with the thesis of non-attachment. Those who believe in the theory of non-attachment or *niṣkāma karma* as means for getting liberation hold the view that the real cause of bondage is attachment and the notion of attachment involves in it the notion of desire but not action and its result which the doctrine of *karma* advocates. If it is the attachment that causes bondage, it causes bondage no matter whether it is attachment to action or to the consequences of action; whether it is done in self-interest or other's interest or in the interest of all; whether it is performed in interested manner or disinterested manner. All cases of attachment would be the cases of bondage which the *karmavādins* do not hold consistently. To make room for liberation they exclude the desire of *mokṣa* or attachment to *mokṣa* from the category of the binding forces of desire, which they cannot do without holding inconsistent view. The prescriptions of non-attached actions as means to obtain freedom or liberation, conflict with the general claim of the doctrine of *karma* that every action entitles its doer to get its result. If every action entitles its doer to get the result of it, he would inevitably get it, no matter whether it is done in attached manner or detached manner. The binding force of *karma* lies in the act of *karma* and its result and not in the manner in which it is done. The *karmavādins* believe in the beginningless process of the transmigration of soul but do not hold the view that transmigration of soul is endless. If bondage is due to *karma*, then liberation is possible only through the stoppage of *karma* and not by doing *karma* in attached or detached manner.

Thus, it is quite obvious from the above analysis that those who believe in the theory of transmigration and consider ignorance and attachment as the causes of bondage their accounts fail to provide a satisfactory explanation or justification. Even if it is accepted for the sake of argument that the theory of transmigration provides a sound explanation and justification for human sufferings, there is no evidence or proof to establish that this doctrine is true and actually operates in human life, nor do we have any evidence or proof for the existence of immortal transmigrating soul in man.

Notes and References

1. Rajendra Prasad, *Karma Causation and Retributive Morality*, Munshiram Manoharlal Publishers Pvt. Ltd., New Delhi, 1989, p. 225.
2. M. Hiriyanna, *The Essentials of Indian Philosophy*, Allen and Unwin, India, 1973, p. 47.
3. Eliot Deutsch, *Advaita Vedānta*, The University Press of Hawaii, Honolulu, 1973, p. 68.
4. Arthur L. Herman, *The Problem of Evil and Indian Thought*, Motilal Banarsidass, First Edition : Delhi, 1976, pp. 146-47.
5. *Sāṁkhya-Kārikā*, 62.
6. Gautama, *Nyāya Darshana*, III. i. 4 ; pp. 716-25 and IV. i. 19-21, pp. 940-57.
7. David Hume, *A Treatise of Human Nature*, ed. L.A. Selby-Bigge (Oxford : Clarendon Press, 1888, 1964), I, iv, 6, p. 251.
8. *Bhagavadgītā*, *Sāṁkhyayoga*, 20.
9. *Ibid.*, 22.
10. *Brihadāraṇyaka*, 1, 5, 17 and *Kauṣītaki*, II, 15.
11. *Manusmriti*, IV, 170.

6

Karma and Divine Intervention

As we have already mentioned in the preceding chapters that there are two different versions of the doctrine of *karma* : theistic and non-theistic. A non-theistic version of the doctrine of *karma* maintains the view that the doctrine of *karma* does not essentially involve in it a reference to God. It is an impersonal doctrine. It does not depend on any divine power. It works by itself in its own natural manner. A monistic and self-centric interpretation of the doctrine of *karma* of the Jainas could be said is a non-theistic version of the doctrine of *karma* because the monistic and self-centric model or interpretation of the Jainas does not assume God, a divine power, as a moral administrator of the law of *karma.* Without assuming the existence of God it interprets the phenomena of *karma* by assuming the existence of the agent who performs actions and is subject to the law of *karma.* The Jainas monistic interpretation of the doctrine of *karma* attributes everything good or bad one has or will ever have to only one kind of causes i.e., to agent and his actions, which the experience does not seem to support. Those who believe in the monistic interpretation of the doctrine of *karma* of Jainism hold the view that the doctrine of *karma* works in an inviolable manner and everyone who performs actions is subject to the law, which means that no agent is above the law of *karma.* Although the Jainas monistic version of the doctrine of *karma* is a non-theistic interpretation but it is not the only non-theistic interpretation of the doctrine of *karma.* There are other non-theistic interpretations of the doctrine of *karma* too in the classical Indian systems of thought. For example, the Buddhists interpretation of the doctrine of *karma* is also a kind of non-theistic version of the doctrine of *karma* in the defined sense of the term 'theistic' but it is not a monistic model or interpretation of the doctrine of *karma,* because it does not attribute everything good or bad to only kind of causes, that is, the agent and his actions. Buddhism believes in the possibility of *kṛtapraṇāśa,* and *akṛtābhyāgama prasaṅgas* which the monistic theory of *karma* denies. The Buddhists do not maintain the thesis that the *karma* is governed by a divine moral administrator i.e., God. On their account, God does not evaluate the moral worth of our action, nor does He decide what we deserve or do not deserve on the basis of our deeds. In fact, they do not believe in the existence of God at all. Hence, for them the question of God's awarding reward and punishment in the forms of happiness and pain respectively on the basis of the deeds does not arise at all. According to them, the function of *karma* does not stand in the need of any external agency. The act force which produces a result lies in the act itself. Thus, on the Buddhists view, the doctrine of *karma* is an autonomous doctrine. In fact, the Buddhists do not associate the notion of *karma* with any notion of permanent, eternal, conscious agency; nor do they believe in the existence of it. They explain the phenomena of action in terms of psycho-physical elements. But those who believe in the theistic version of the doctrine of *karma,* unlike Buddhism, Jainism, Sāṁkhya, Mīmāṁsā, maintain the view that the doctrine of *karma* essentially depends on the divine power for its operation. According to them, the doctrine of *karma* is a doctrine of moral administrator of the world who is none other than God. For them, it is God who decides what we deserve or do not deserve on the account of our deeds. In their view, God does not only evaluate our actions in terms of merit and demerit but also awards to us our dues. It is believed that God awards reward when we do good deeds and punishment when we do bad deeds. But what is good or bad? On this question the theistic *karmavādins* have different opinions. The theistic interpretation of the doctrine of *karma* assumes the belief in the existence of God, over and above the belief in the existence of human agency or the agency of self. Those who hold the theistic version of the doctrine of *karma,* like Rāmānuja and some Naiyāyikas, are of the opinion that the doctrine of *karma* cannot work by itself. They believe in the existence of God as mediator between act and its result. Not only this, they also believe that liberation from the chain of births, deaths and rebirths cannot be obtained through knowledge and action alone unless we obtain the grace of God. Although the opinions of the theistic *karmavādins* differ as regard to the nature of God and the state of liberation, but by and large they all believe besides acquisition of right knowledge and performance of non-attached action the acquisition of grace is also essentially required to make one's ownself free from its *karmic* bondage including ignorance. It is of their opinion that if God is happy, He will liberate us from all sins and sufferings. As it is said in the *Gītā*, "Abandoning all other principles, take refuge in Me alone. I will deliver you from all sin; do not grieve."[1] The similar view has been expressed in the *Upaniṣads* also, "The self cannot be gained by knowledge, not by understanding, not by learning. It may be gained only by him to whom the God chooses."[2] God lifts up His devotees from the ocean of births, deaths and rebirths. Though the theistic *karmavādins* by and large believe in the existence of God and think that He is omniscient, omnipotent, omnipresent and benevolent in nature but they hold the view that He Himself does not create evils in the life of human beings or any other beings for that matter. They do not hold God responsible for the existence of miseries and sufferings in the universe. In their opinion, God is mere maintainer of the records of good and bad deeds performed by the doers and on the basis of their records He awards rewards and punishments in the forms of happiness and pain. For them, it is the agent who is responsible for everything, whatsoever happens in his or her life and not God. They explain and justify sins by referring to the agent and his actions without assuming the existence of God as a creator of sins. So far we have analysed and examined the non-theistic versions of *karma* and have drawn certain conclusions arising from it in the previous chapters. In this chapter, therefore, we will confine our discussions with the theistic interpretation of the doctrine of *karma* which has not been emphasized very much in the modern writings and will bring out certain philosophical issues involved in it. Generally it is the non-theistic version of the doctrine of *karma* which is taken as the distinctive feature of the classical Indian philosophy. But this does not mean that it is held by all the classical schools of Indian philosophy; nor does it mean that those who associate the notion of divine being with the doctrine of *karma*, their account is insignificant and does not form a part of philosophical, cultural and religious trends of India. The theistic version of the doctrine of *karma* is present as much as the monistic version of the doctrine of *karma* in our philosophical, cultural and religious traditions.

When we reflect critically on the theistic version of the doctrine of *karma,* we find by and large that it is based on the assumptions that there exists a God who is eternal, omniscient, omnipresent, omnipotent, benevolent, immanent, controller, creator, sustainer, destroyer, preserver, maintainer, transcendental, unbound, above the law of *karma,* perfect, embodiment of good qualities and the object of devotion. He is conceived not only above the law of *karma* but also the author of the law of *karma* in the sense that the law of *karma* originates from Him and does not have its own ontological independent existence. He is believed to have a power to administer and revoke it. But these assumptions, instead of solving the problem of *karma* connected with individuals and their actions, create more problems because of essentially involving the belief in the existence of God.

The theistic *karmavādins* have made considerable efforts and spent energy in constructing arguments for the existence of God. Not only the theistic *karmavādins* but also philosophers and theologicians, both Eastern and Western, have been busy since beginning either polishing and revising whole arguments offered for the existence of God or constructing new ones for proving the existence of God. But the fact remains that all purported proofs for the existence of God are nothing but rationalizations producing the illusion that one has a rational basis for holding the belief that there exists God. This is not only true in regard to the proofs for the existence of God but also in regard to the proofs for the functioning of the doctrine of *karma* as well in which both the theistic and the non-theistic *karmavādins* believe. When we reflect on the theistic accounts of God, no matter whether it is Hinduism or Christianity or Islam, we find that they do not hold the same conception of God. They use the same word 'God' but give different meanings to it in their moral, religious and cultural systems. In other words, we find that there are different conceptions of God in different religions and cultures and each theist while giving the proofs for the existence of God, gives impressions as if he is proving the existence of same God. While the fact is that his conception of God and the proofs offered for the existence of God is religion and culture bound. Not only this, the propositions which the theists use as premises to establish the conclusion that God exists are highly ambiguous, and without establishing the truth of the propositions they draw the conclusion that God exists and think that they have proved it. While the fact is that their arguments for the existence of God prove nothing about God's existence except that they have certain conceptions of God. And their different conceptions of God prove that God exists only in their conceptions and not outside of them which means, in other words, God exists in human minds and not independent of them, as it is claimed. Human beings create the conception of God through their minds and then start proving the existence of God that He exists independent of them and is the supreme being. This fact is quite obvious from their different conceptions of God themselves, because they attribute incompatible properties to God which are logically impossible to do. Not only their conception of God differs but also the proofs offered for the existence of God differ. While proving the existence of God they reject each other's argument offered in favour of the existence of God. For example, Rāmānuja rejects Naiyāyikas arguments and Naiyāyikas reject Rāmānuja' s arguments, which suggests that no one has authentic evidence for the existence of God, no matter how He is conceived. Those who believe in the existence of God do not establish their basic propositions from which they draw the conclusion of the existence of God. Unless the truth of the basic premises from which the conclusion of the existence of God is drawn are not established, the theists are not entitled to make the claim that they have evidences or proofs for the existence of God; nor do they can establish that the doctrine of *karma* is dependent on God for its operation, since the latter is conceived to be originating from the former. No matter what and how many arguments we put forward for the existence of God, we prove nothing about the existence of God unless the basic premises of arguments are proved true, which the theists have not done and if at all they have done, their proofs are bound to suffer from logical weaknesses. Those who failed to provide good reasons in support of the existence of God appeal to faith and make the claim that God is not the subject matter of arguments but is the matter of faith, which indicates that they do not have distinct and clear knowledge of God. If at all God exists, in what sense does He exist? Even on this question we find that the theists have different opinions. Some of them are of the view that God does not exist like body in space and time, while others believe that God does have a divine body. But in what sense God does have a divine body, it seems they themselves are not very clear when we go into their conception of divine body itself. If nobody can be conceived, given its nature, without conceiving the existence of space and time, how can a divine body being one of the species of body falls outside or transcendents spatio-temporal conditions. If God is existing, He must be existing somewhere at some time. If at all God is existing, He must have been the object of knowledge of who claim about His existence. And if this is so, their knowledge about God should have not been different unless there are different Gods. And if there are different Gods, at least those those who belong to the same religion and culture their accounts should have not been different. But this is not the case. As we have already pointed out that their opinion about God is different, from which it follows that they do not have the same conception of God within the same religio-cultural system and creates doubt about the existence of God. All the proofs so far given for the existence of God, when we go into their analysis, we find that they suffer from certain shortcomings, no matter whether they are scriptural proofs (i.e., *Vedic* or non-*Vedic*) or cosmological proof, or teleological proof or any other proof for that matter. The existence of God can never be proved on the basis of the arguments because the truth of their premises always stand in need of some epistemic and ontic grounds other than the logical arguments. When we go into the history of different religions, we find that they say different things and do not hold the same view about God, what to say of His existence within or without the realm of one's own religion and culture.

Let us assume for our purpose that the theistic *karmavādins* postulate that God exists is true and then see whether their characterizations of God do conflict with the general *karmic* beliefs or not. The theistic *karmavādins* believe that God acts as a mediator between the *karmic* agent and his *karmas* in the sense that it is the God who maintains the records of merit and demerit of the individuals who perform actions and awards rewards and punishments in the forms of happiness and pain respectively according to their deeds. In fact in their view, the law of *karma* cannot function without God. They are of the opinion that God is the moral governor of the universe. He maintains moral ecology by upholding the law of *karma*. On their account, God not only upholds the law but also is the authority of the law. He maintains justice in the universe by applying the law of *karma*. He does not inflict sufferings upon the individuals arbitrarily at His sweet will. Sufferings are inflicted upon the individuals according to their demerits which they themselves acquire through their deeds. God is not conceived as the creator of evils. Individuals themselves earn evils through their deeds. Thus on their opinion, God cannot be condemned on the ground of the existence of evils (i.e., sufferings) found in the universe, no matter whether the discourse of the universe is a discourse of human beings or other beings. But, in their view, God has power to revoke the law of *karma,* if he chooses, and can grant liberation to the individuals who sincerely worship Him in detached spirit or disinterested manner from the bondage of *karma* or from the cycle of births, deaths and rebirths through His grace. In fact, those who believe that the notion of God is essentially connected with the doctrine of *karma* think by and large that without God's grace liberation (*mokṣa*) is not possible at all, even if we perform actions with right knowledge and in detached manner. In other words, according to them, liberation is possible only through God's grace and to obtain God's grace, the devotion of God is essential. It is believed that one who worships God sincerely in disinterested manner God, out of love, compassion or benevolence liberates him from all sorts of sufferings and sins. In support of their thesis different instances are quoted from various scriptures like *Upaniṣads, Gītā, Rāmāyaṇa, Śrī Bhāgavata* etc. where by the grace of God, it is believed, certain persons were granted either salvation or abode in the heavens. The giant vulture Jatāyu,[3] the virtuous aboriginal woman Śabarī[4], the ape-king Sugrīva,[5] and Ajāmila[6] are the famous instances in this regard. But one who gets liberation by the grace of God, the *karmavādins,* like Rāmānuja, believe that he does not become identical with God. He only becomes similar to God in respect of certain characteristics. The theistic *karmavādins* always give supremacy to their respective Gods but not to the law of *karma.* They also do not give equal status to the liberated individuals which they give to God. But when we examine their account of God's grace in connection with the doctrine of *karma* and its beliefs embodied in it, we find that their account of God's grace conflicts with the assertions of the doctrine of *karma.* The doctrine of *karma,* as we have already pointed out in the earlier chapters, asserts that every action produces some pleasure or pain which and only which its doer is bound to experience in the present or next life because he deserves them. This binding force lies in the mechanism of act itself performed by the individuals and not in any external agency, divine or human. And these assertions of the doctrine of *karma* rule out the possibility of God's intervention. How the *karmic* assertions rule out the logical possibility of God's intervention can be seen in the following way :

If God is the immanent controller of everything, He is also the immanent controller of all human activities and actions. If God is the immanent controller of all human activities and action then human activities and actions are not within the power of them. They are rather within the power of God and it is God who originates them. If it is not within the power of human beings to change their courses of events without the involvement of God's grace and intervention then they cannot be said to be the maker of their own fate. Their fate is, in fact, determined by God. God is the maker of their destiny. Whatever human beings do, good or bad, do, not because they choose them but because they are fated by God to do so. If this position is correct, then human beings should not, and cannot, be held morally responsible, as they are held by the theistic *karmavādins,* on the account of whatever they do in their life journey. In fact, it is God who should be held responsible for everything that happens in their life because it is He who immanently does everything. Human beings do not do anything on their own. They are rather made by God to do so. They are mere instruments of God in the sense that through them God performs His activities. They do not play any active role in regard to the happenings in their life. In fact, human beings do not have any freedom. Even if they wish, they cannot play any active role independent of God in the origination of action. Since everything is controlled by God and God is the immanent doer on the theistic account, human beings cannot make their destiny through their deeds without God's will. Human beings do not have power to control over their activities. Actions are not in their power to perform or not to perform at their free will, since they lack free will. And if human beings are not free in performing actions and their activities are monitored by God, how can they be held morally responsible on account of the deeds which they perform in their life? Human beings can be held morally responsible for their sufferings and miseries on the account of their deeds only when we presume that they have power to do them freely independent of God's intervention. If they do not do anything freely by themselves, they do not earn anything; and if they do not earn anything, they cannot be held to be deserving something because deserving of something always presupposes earning of it. Moral responsibility consists in the agent's free actions and not in his unfree actions. Therefore on this ground it is God who should be held responsible because it is He who performs actions freely. To say that God is the immanent controller and the doer of everything that happens in the universe is to say that it is God who determines and ordains all that happens in human life. But to accept this view amounts to contradicting the *karmic* beliefs embodied in the doctrine of *karma* because according to the doctrine of *karma* human beings are the maker of their own fate and none else. They themselves determine their fate through their deeds. Since human beings are thought to be the maker of their own fate, they are also held morally responsible for whatever happens in their life, good or bad, on the account of their deeds and not anyone else, human or divine. This *karmic* belief is held on the assumption that human beings do have power to change the courses of their events. They have power of choosing and causing certain actions by their free will. Since they are believed to have power to change the courses of events, they are called the maker of their fate according to their choice. If they decide to be free they can make themselves free from the chain of *karmic* bondage by removing the courses of bondage and regain the soul's original position. This *karmic* belief which the *karmavādins* hold cannot be said to be the consequence of the doctrine of fatalism and divine determinism; nor can it be said to be the consequence of the determinism of the nature (*prakṛti*). The choosing power which human beings possess does not come from any external agency human or divine. It is an internal power. It comes from the individual's own self. The individual self in the *karmic* paradigm is assumed to have tremendous infinite autonomous power in its essence, not only to change the courses of events but also to transcend them. Human beings are conceived not merely as the victim of their fate, no matter whether its source is *karma* or divine but also are believed to be the maker of their fate through their deeds. This *karmic* belief is opposed to divine determinism and intervention. The theistic *karmavādins* cannot hold both the accounts, as they do, consistently since they are incompatible. The theistic version of the doctrine of *karma* suffers from internal inconsistencies, not only with regard to God's grace and intervention but also with regard to their some other beliefs associated with God and *karma.* If God performs action, how can He be free from the result of action arising from it according to the doctrine of *karma* ? If the doctrine of *karma* is a valid doctrine, it must be valid not only in the context of human actions but also in the context of divine actions being the doctrine of action. It must hold good in all the cases of action in spite of their differences and originations. If it holds good in some cases of action and does not hold good in some other cases of action, no matter what they are and from where they originate, it cannot be said to be universally and objectively valid. The theistic *karmavādins* on the one hand characterize God as the immanent doer of everything and human beings are treated as mere instruments but on the other hand when the question of responsibility attached to action comes, they do not want to hold God responsible on the account of what human beings do, good or bad. On their account, God does everything but He is above the consequences of action. They associate sufferings resulting from His actions to human beings, which they should not have done according to the doctrine of *karma*. Because according to the doctrine of *karma*, the fruit of action must be realized by its doer and not by anyone else and he should be held responsible for it, which the *karmavādins* do not hold in the respect of God due to their religious prejudices. Instead of holding God responsible, they hold human beings responsible for God's actions and make God free from the *karmic* bondage by conceiving Him above the law of *karma.* In their view, God performs actions but is not governed by the doctrine of *karma.* The doctrine of *karma* in their view, has its validity only in the context of human actions but not in the context of God's actions which is unjustified. If human beings do not perform actions, they are not in fact governed by the law of *karma.* It is God who should be governed by the law of *karma* because it is He who performs actions and not human beings. One who deserves *karmic* penalty does not get it and one who does not deserve gets it which the doctrine of *karma* does not allow. The doctrine of *karma* does not admit exceptions, neither in favour of God nor in favour of human beings, as the theistic *karmavādins* advocate. Because what constitutes as a ground in the case of human beings according to the doctrine of *karma,* also constitutes as a ground in the case of God. Any one who performs action automatically comes by virtue of his performing action under the jurisdiction of the doctrine of *karma,* if it is valid. No doer is above the doctrine of *karma.* But the theistic *karmavādins* on this question do not hold a consistent view. They believe that God is the immanent doer of everything but do not believe that He is governed by the doctrine of *karma.* They conceive Him that He is above the law of *karma* which they should not have done in order to maintain the consistency of their *karmic* theory. They should not have made exception to the law of *karma* in favour of God in the formulation of their theory of *karma.* If God Himself violates the doctrine of *karma* in favour of His own devotees by granting grace to him, how can He be the moral governor of the universe ? To make exception to the law of *karma* in favour of His own devotees amounts to violating the law of *karma* and to violate the law of *karma* is to commit a moral crime. If God Himself violates the law, then that means He does not act on principle and one who does not act on principle is not morally praiseworthy. The upholder of the law of *karma* is not supposed to violate it. He rather is supposed to honour it being the authority of the law. But instead of honouring the law God breaks the law and thereby disturbs moral equilibrium. If He breaks the law in favour of His devotees because of His emotional weakness towards His devotees, He is not a perfect being, as the theistic *karmavādins* conceive. He is in this regard on par with human beings. If God is perfect then He must act on principle and should not break it in favour of anyone, whether he is His devotee or not, in order to maintain moral harmony in the universe and provide justice to all His creatures according to their deeds, or else, he would cease to be the moral governor and the maintainer of the universe. If it is the characteristics of the law of *karma* that it is immutable and inviolable then no one including God can escape from it. This is analytically true. Whosoever performs action becomes bound to realize the consequences of action. If God, as the theistic *karmavādins* believe, can escape us by revoking the law of *karma* then to characterize the law of *karma* as immutable and inviolable is a mistake because the notions of immutability and inviolability rule out the possibility of escaping from it. If there is a way of escaping from the law of *karma* then the theistic *karmavādins* cannot claim with the authority, as they do, that whatever we do, sooner or later, brings to us the result we merit and there is no way of escaping from it. Not only this, if the law of *karma* is immutable and inviolable and its immutability and inviolability constitute its nature then these characteristics of the law of *karma* rule out the possibility of the intervention of God. Even if God wishes to intervene, He cannot do it. His efforts would be futile. If God due to His mighty power can manipulate with the *karmic* mechanism in order to give grace to His devotees which the law itself does not permit, why does He not do it in the cases of non-devotees ? Being a kind person He should grant grace to all His creatures to liberate them from sufferings and miseries. If God is omnipotent and benevolent, He could have avoided the whole drama of the creation and eliminated sufferings from human and non-human life. If He did not wish to eliminate sufferings, how can He be benevolent, kind and good ? If the elimination of sufferings is beyond His power, He is not omnipotent. The existence of suffering goes against God's characteristics. If we are bound by our deeds to get reward and punishment in the forms of happiness and pain respectively then there is no necessity of God. Not only this, morally He is also not supposed to intervene in the *karmic* process. If the getting of *karmic* reward and punishment is built in the internal mechanism of *karma* itself, God's role becomes superfluous. If God's revoking of law is justified on the ground of the service renders towards Him then He is not a benevolent because it would amount to mean that He is a selfish but is not kind and generous. He gives grace only to those who work for Him. He acts on the principle of utility and that goes against His characteristics of benevolence and kindness. It cannot be said, as it is said in the *Gītā*,[7] that God created four *varṇas* on the basis of their deeds because the creation of human existence comes logically prior to the performance of their deeds and what comes logically prior to cannot be justified or established on the basis of that what comes later to it. The theistic *karmavādins* version of the doctrine of *karma*, in fact, conflicts with their characterization of God. Their account suffers from all sorts of disadvantages and inconsistencies from which the theological ethics suffers being its one of the species. By assuming the God's intervention and grace, the theistic *karmavādins* instead of solving the *karmic* problems create more problems. Even on the issue of the relationship of God and soul which human beings in their opinion possess, the theistic *karmavādin's* accounts conflict. They not only hold different views but also conflicting views about the nature and relation of God and soul, and when we go into their accounts, we find that their metaphysical accounts of God and soul conflict with their ethical *karmic* accounts. For example, according to Rāmānuja[8] God is an organic unity of soul and body. God, soul and body are inseparably connected. Soul and body are dependent on God but God is not dependent on them. On his account, God, soul and body are three ultimate realities. In fact, he does not maintain consistency with regard to the relation of God and soul. Sometimes, he says, the soul is a part of God, sometimes, the body of God, sometimes, a mode of God, sometimes, an attribute or qualification of God and sometimes, as absolutely dependent on God and controlled, supported and utilized by God. If soul and body are inseparably connected with God and God also is inseparably connected with them then how can God be free from sufferings, miseries and changes and be above the law of *karma*? If God is the immanent soul of the universe then how can He be at the same time transcendental? If God, soul and body are inseparably connected, it makes no sense to say on the basis of it that soul and body are dependent on God and God is not dependent on them. If God is immanent in our soul and body then worshipping of God would amount to worshipping of ourselves and that is absurd. And it makes no sense to maintain the distinction between devotee and devoted. If the body of God is made up of *prakṛti* and souls, and *prakṛti* consists of *sattva, raja* and *tama* then how can God be free from the effects of the *guṇas* of *prakṛti* and be above the law of causation. If the soul is essentially pure, changeless and self-conscious subject, why should it get associated with *karma* and be bound? If pure, changeless and self-conscious entity (like soul) can get associated with *karma* and be bound, why is it not possible in regard to God Himself? We cannot argue on this ground that the association of self with *karma* is possible because it is finite and this is not possible in the case of God because God is infinite, because finity and infinity do not have anything to do with their association with ignorance. The self gets associated with *karma* according to the *karmavādins* not on the ground that it is finite but on the ground of its ignorance and how did it happen in the beginning, on this question Rāmānuja has no satisfactory answer. If bondage is because of ignorance, its removal, as Saṁkara rightly says, is possible only by knowledge and not by devotion, as Rāmānuja advocates. Devotion, like *niṣkāma karma*, is also a kind of action and in order to reap or realize its result, the devotee, according to the law of *karma*, is bound to take birth. If this be so, how can the devotee get liberation from the chain of births, deaths and rebirths through devotion? Devotional actions, instead of making the devotee free, bind him.

The Nyāya-Vaiśeṣika version of the doctrine of *karma* does not suffer from the above mentioned difficulties from which Rāmānuja's account suffers because their metaphysical accounts of God, soul, body and their relation are different. But to say this does not mean that their theistic account of the doctrine of *karma* is valid and free from shortcomings. Their account of the doctrine of *karma* too suffers from some other sorts of difficulties. For example, if the soul is in its essence devoid of consciousness then how can it get associated and influenced by ignorance ? Only a conscious being can be conceived to be affected by ignorance which, in their view, self is not. The Nyāya-Vaiśeṣika holds the view that God is the creator of the world but He is disembodied. If God is disembodied then how can He be a *kartā* ? Because for to be a *kartā*, he must perform actions and actions cannot be performed, as we have already seen in the second chapter, without the involvement of body and bodily muscle contractions. For to be a *kartā* of the world, God must have a body. Not only this, to govern the universe and to maintain the moral equilibrium on the basis of the deeds of the individuals, He must have a physical body which, on the account of Nyāya-Vaiśeṣika, He does not have. The use of the notion of *kartṛtva* always involves in it a reference to body according to our analysis of action. If both God and self, on their account, are *kartās* then how is it that only self gets associated with *karma* but not God? On this question the Nyāya-Vaiśeṣika does not have any answer. On the one hand, they conceive God as a *kartā* but, on the other hand, they conceive Him as free from the *karmic* bondage which is inconsistent. If God performs action then according to the law of *karma*, He cannot be above the operation of it. If God is above the domain of *karma*, how can He be characterized as a *kartā*? Because for to be a *kartā*, He is bound to perform action; and if He performs action, He automatically comes under the operation and jurisdiction of the law of *karma*. And from this point of view, He is on par with human beings. If cognition, volition and desire are essentially connected with the notion of *kartā* then God cannot be said to be free from them being a *kartā* and their relation would remain the same, no matter whether the *kartā* is finite or infinite.

From the foregoing discussions, thus, we find that the theistic version of the doctrine of *karma*, no matter what its version is, suffers from a lot of philosophical difficulties because of which it fails to provide a satisfactory explanation as regard to the existence of sufferings found in the human and non-human world. The theistic interpretation of the doctrine of *karma* does not stand to reasons.

Notes and References

1. *Bhagavadgītā*, *Mokṣayoga*, 66.
2. *Cf. Kaṭhopaniṣad*, 1.2.23.
3. *Vālmīki Rāmāyaṇa*, *Araṇyakāṇḍa*, 68, 29-31.
4. *Ibid.*, 68, 31-33.
5. *Vālmīki Rāmāyaṇa*, *Uttarakāṇḍa*, 108, 25-26.
6. *Śrībhāgavata*, 6, 1-2.
7. *Bhagavadgītā*, *Jnānayoga*, 13.
8. C.D. Sharma, *A Critical Survey of Indian Philosophy*, Motilal Banarsidass.

7

Conclusion

We find out in our analysis that the notion of *karma* is essentially connected with the notion of agency, a conscious being, who is believed to have powers not only of causing or not causing *karmas* on certain occasions but also is thought to be the locus of all conscious activities like the activities of thinking, experiencing, believing, reasoning, understanding, intending, desiring, willing, choosing, deliberating, planning, transcendenting etc. with which the notion of *karma* is associated. So without assuming the existence of a conscious agency, no *karma* can be conceived to be possible because what makes it possible is the conscious agency. The notion of *karma* is conceptually related with the notion of *kriyā* (activity) and the notion of *kriyā* is conceptually related with the notion of agent (*kartā*). The *karma* without the *kriyā* is not possible and the *kriyā* without the *kartā* is not conceivable. But from this we should not infer that the notion of *kartā* has a causal meaning in isolation of the notion of *karma*. The notion of *kartā* has no causal meaning in isolation of the notion of *karma*. The notion of *kartā* is causally linked with the notion of *karma* and the notion of *karma* is causally linked with the notion of *kartā* because of which the understanding of one is not possible without making a reference to the other. A man becomes *kartā* just by doing *karma*. Nobody becomes a *kartā* without performing *karma*. The conceptual connection which is found between the notions of *kartā* and *karma* is built in their causal structural meanings themselves because of which an intelligible use of the notion of *kartā* is not possible without making a reference to the notion of *karma* and so is the case vice versa. A meaningful use of the notion of *karma* always involves a reference to the notion of *kartā*. From this point of view, we can say that the notion of *karma* is different from the notion of event. Events just happen under the presence of certain antecedent conditions without involving the role of any conscious agency while the *karmas* are always done and brought about through conscious efforts and activities. That is the reason why the occurrences of action are called the occurrences of conscious phenomena unlike the occurrences of the events of physical, chemical and biological phenomena. The theistic *karmavādins* who regard all the events as the deeds of God nullify the class of events. For them, there is no such entity called as an event. What we generally call as events, they call them as the acts of God. Theistic *karmavādins* in fact do not maintain any logical distinction between the notions of event and action which in our opinion rests on a logical mistake. Because both the notions belong to two different logical categories and hence to identify one with another would amount to the committing a fallacy of the category-mistake. The notion of action is essentially linked with the notion of a conscious agency with which the notion of event is not essentially linked. Since the notion of event is not essentially linked with the notion of a conscious agency; therefore it is possible for us to understand and explain the notion of event without making any reference to the notion of any conscious agency. In other words, we can meaningfully use the notion of event without assuming the ontological existence of any conscious agency behind it which is not logically possible in the respect of the notion of *karma* because of its conceptual affinity with the notion of a conscious agency.

The notion of *kartā* can be viewed from two different angles : metaphysical and functional. From the metaphysical point of view, we can say that a *kartā* (agent) is what he is in himself apart from and independent of his relation to *karma* and the things causally affected by it. But from the functional point of view, a *kartā* is what he does or how he affects other things through his *karma*. For a *kartā* to act means to come into a causal relation to *karma* and the things affected by it. The causal relation that holds between *kartā* and *karma* also holds between *karma* and *karma phala,* and *kartā* and *karma phala*. From the causal point of view, we can say that *kartā, karma* and *karma phala* are relative terms. Since a causal relation is not a reciprocal or two directional relation, we cannot legitimately say that what is caused by something also causes that thing. What causes need not be caused and what is caused need not cause something. This is perfectly quite possible. But to say this does not mean that what is a cause in relation to one thing cannot be an effect in relation to another thing. However there are three logical possibilities so far the *karmic* effects are concerned. The *karmas* of *kartā* can either affect the *kartā* himself or the other things external to the *kartā* or both the *kartā* as well as the other things, conscious or unconscious. So far the classical Indian tradition is concerned, we find out that there are two different views about the possibility of the *karmic* effects, which may be called as monistic and non-monistic views of the *karmavādins*. Those *karmavādins* who hold monistic version of the doctrine of *karma* maintain the view that only the doer of *karma* gets affected by the *karma* and none else which empirical experiences do not seem to support. But those who hold non-monistic version of the doctrine of *karma* like Buddhism maintain the view that the doer of *karma* may or may not be affected by his *karma* or a person may be affected by certain *karmas* which may not be his *karmas* at all. This account of *karma*, no doubt, is a factually sound account but is not a morally sound account, because morality does not allow it. According to it, the result of *karma* must be realized by the doer of *karma* because he earns it by doing the *karma* and what he earns, he deserves it; and what he deserves, he must get it. This means that one who does not perform *karma* does not owe the result of *karma* and what he does not owe, he must not get it. A morally sound *karmic* theory does not allow the logical possibility of *kṛtapraṇāśa* and *akṛtābhyāgama* which the Buddhists account allows. And hence the Buddhists account of the doctrine of *karma* cannot be said to be a morally sound account within the framework of the *karmic* system. Although the monistic version of the doctrine of *karma* is a morally sound doctrine within the framework of the *karmic* system, but it rules out the possibility of moral, social, religious and cultural interpersonal human interactions to which the monistic *karmavādins* themselves would not like to subscribe. In fact, they also do not subscribe to it in certain contexts of interpersonal human interaction *i.e., śrāddha, riṇa, varṇa* duties.

If we admit for the sake of argument that a *kartā* is analysable in terms of what he does without assuming of its beinghood, then what the doctrine of *karma* asserts becomes meaningless and absurd because what it asserts always involves in it a reference to some conscious agency, that is, a substantive conscious being who is conceived as different not only from *karma* but also is thought to be its originator. So, for to make the *karmic* assertions meaningful, the *karmavādins* are logically bound to maintain the distinction between the notions of *kartā* and *karma.* Reducing one to the other would amount to not only committing the fallacy of a category-mistake, but also making the assertions of the doctrine of *karma* meaningless and absurd. But to maintain the distinction between them does not entitle us to infer doing of something from the *kartā's* beinghood. Because to be is not to do or to exist is not always to act. Existence without doing is possible but doing without existence is not possible; from which it follows that the way in which the notion of doing is related to the notion of existence, the notion of existence is not related in that way to the notion of doing. The notion of doing is necessarily linked with the notion of existence, but the notion of existence is not necessarily linked with the notion of doing. If this view is true, a *kartā* can ontologically be conceived to be existing even when he does not do any *karma* because the notions of existence and beinghood are not essentially connected with the notion of doing while the notion of doing is essentially connected with them. If a *kartā* does not act, from this it does not follow that he does not exist. In this respect what is true of *kartā* is also true of *karma* and *karma phala. Karma* and *karma phala* can be conceived to be existing from the ontological point of view even when they do not affect other things. Because what comes ontologically prior to can be said to be existing independent of what comes ontologically later to it. As a matter of fact, there are many things in the universe which exist but do not perform any sort of *karma* nor can they legitimately be said to have the capacities of playing the role of a *karmic* agency. For example, material bodies, animals, insects and birds etc. no doubt do exist in the universe but they do not perform any sort of *karma.* Material bodies and psychophysical events are devoid of consciousness and hence cannot play the role of a *karmic* agency. In their contexts the notions of *kartā* and *karma* do not have intelligible applicability. As far as animals, insects and birds are concerned, no doubt they are not devoid of consciousness. But they too are not believed on the basis of the scientific evidences that they have *karmic* agential capacities—the capacities which are required for bringing about the *karmas* like thinking, reasoning, analysing, understanding, experiencing, believing, intending, deliberating, choosing, planning, willing, desiring etc. And therefore in their contexts too the question of their performing of *karma* simply does not arise at all. If they do not perform *karmas*, they cannot legitimately be said to be affected by their *karmas*, from which it does not follow that they cannot be affected by the *karmas* of others. The *karmas* of human beings, no doubt do affect them but that would be quite a different thing from that of saying that they are affected by their *karmas*, as the *karmavādins* believe. Even if for the sake of argument it is accepted that they have the *karmic* capacities and are governed by the law of *karma*, it does not refute the thesis that to be is not to do or to exist is not always to act or a *kartā* cannot ontologically be conceived to be existing without being causally related to *karma* and the things affected by it.

Perhaps human beings are the only beings who can legitimately be said to have the *karmic* agential capacities of bringing something about. So only in their contexts the intelligibility of the doctrine of *karma* and its assertions can be judged and examined. Although human beings are believed to have the agential powers to cause or not to cause certain *karmas* but they may not execute them in bringing certain *karmas* about or refraining from them. But on that ground of the potential capacities they cannot legitimately be characterized as *kartā*, because no one becomes a *kartā* just on the basis of the potential agential powers unless he executes them in bringing about certain actions. Animals, insects and birds etc. can be said to have agential powers on the basis of the belief is the existence of self associated with their bodies as the Jaina *karmavādins* say, but on the basis of that they cannot be said to be performing actions unless they execute them in bringing about actions or refraining from them, which empirical experiences do not seem to support. Having a power is one thing and executing of that power is another thing and both the notions are logically unconnected, since somebody may be conceived to have an agential power even when he does not execute it. Actions occur when the agential powers are executed and the execution of agential powers either in bringing about actions or refraining from them always requires on the part of agent to make some conscious efforts and activities associated with actions which are not empirically possible, and may be even logically too, without assuming the unity of a conscious entity (i.e., self) and body. Because it is the body through which agential powers are executed and manifested directly or indirectly. But assuming of this would amount to admitting that *karma* is not the cause of the unity of self and body, as the *karmavādins* believe since the unity of self and body always logically and ontologically comes prior to the performance of *karma.* Physical manifestations no doubt do constitute some empirical basis for us to judge whether somebody is performing conscious activities and actions or not but they do constitute a causal basis being the effects of action. Physical manifestations also do not constitute a logical basis because a person may perform certain conscious activities like the activities of thinking, reasoning, analysing, desiring, willing etc. without manifesting them physically. But thereby we should not infer that bodily ingredients are not causally associated in any form with the origination of action. Body and bodily muscle contractions no doubt (according to our analysis of action) are invariably found involved directly or indirectly in the origination of action because it is body and bodily muscle contractions through which conscious efforts and activities are brought into existence. Even if it is admitted for the sake of argument that the finite and infinite selves are capable of performing actions without being associated with body, material or divine, they cannot be conceived to be free from the *karmic* bondage, because just by performing certain *karma* they automatically come under the operation and jurisdiction of the law of *karma* irrespective of whether they perform *karma* with or without body. Further, though the bodily ingredients are causally connected with *karma* but they cannot be said to be performing the role of a *karmic* agent since they lack some other agential powers which the *karma* requires for its origination. While performing *karma* the agent not only experiences that he is performing *karma* but also feels that it is his *karma* and he is doing it from which the bodily ingredients are devoid of. When the agent performs *karma* freely, he believes that he is responsible for whatever he does and whatever he does freely, he also thinks that he deserves the fruit of it. The agent's beliefs, intentions, desires, and wills etc. no doubt do play some causal roles in the origination of his *karma* but they by themselves do not, and cannot, produce *karma* unless they are carried out by the agent himself. The causal roles of the agent and his beliefs, intentions, desires and wills etc. are not mutually incompatible. Since mental events like intending, wanting, believing etc. cannot by themselves produce *karma* without the agent, the *karmic* phenomena associated with these mental activities cannot be explained and understood solely in terms of them without assuming some metaphysical entity called 'agent' who intends, wants and believes.

So far the relation of *kartā*, *karma* and *karma phala* is concerned, their relation is a causal relation and a causal relation is not a reciprocal or a two directional relation. The *kartā* is causally related to *karma* and the *karma* is causally related to *karma phala* and so is the case vice versa. But the existence of *kartā* is not ontologically dependent upon the existence of *karma* and the existence of *karma* is not ontologically dependent upon the existence of *karma phala*, while the existence of *karma phala* is ontologically dependent upon the existence of *karma* and the existence of *karma* is ontologically dependent upon the existence of *kartā* in the sense that, without presupposing the ontological existence of *kartā*, *karma* is not possible and without presupposing of the ontological existence of *karma* the *karma phala* is not conceivable. For the *karmic* assertions to be meaningful the *karmavādins* are not only required to presuppose that there exists a substantive conscious being who has the agential capacities associated with actions but also to presuppose that the *kartā* and the *bhoktā* (the experiencer of the *karma phala* of *karma*) signify one and the same substantive conscious being who exists and persists at different times and have the power of *kartṛtva* and *bhoktṛtva* and the *karma phala* of *karma* is not destroyed before the realisation by its doer. Unless we presuppose the identity of *kartā* and *bhoktā* and the conservability of *karma phala* till its realisation, we cannot legitimately say that the *karma* entitles its doer some joy or sorrow which he unfailingly or inevitably gets what he is entitled to or deserves. If a *kartā* does not persist at different times, he cannot realise the *karma phala* of his *karma* and in that case *kṛtapraṇāśa* is bound to happen and the *kartā* cannot be a *bhoktā* of the *karma phala* of his *karma* in which the *karmavādins* believe. If the *kartā* is not a *bhoktā*, then someone may likely get some result which may not be the result of any of his *karma* and in that case *akṛtābhyāgama* is bound to happen. Therefore to avoid the unhappy moral situation of *kṛtapraṇāśa* and *akṛtābhyāgama* the identity of *kartā* and *bhoktā* and the conservability of *karma phala* have to be assumed. Any version of the doctrine of *karma* which does not assume the identity of *kartā* and *bhoktā* and the conservability of *karma phala* like Buddhism is bound to be unsatisfactory and morally unintelligible. Further, even if we assume the identity of *kartā* and *bhoktā* and the conservability of *karma phala* of *karma*, from this it does not follow that the doer of good gets good result and the doer of bad gets bad result and no doer gets a reverse result of any of his *karma* unless we again presuppose that the *karma* produces its fitting result, that is, good *karma* produces good result and bad *karma* produces bad result and no good *karma* produces bad result and bad *karma* produces good result. Then and then alone we can legitimately and meaningfully say that the doer of good gets good result and the doer of bad gets bad result and no doer gets reverse result of his *karma.* A man reaps what he sows. But these *karmic* assumptions and assertions cannot be validated on the empirical grounds, nor can they be said to be the result of inductive generalisations from a set of empirical data. They are neither provable nor refutable by means of any evidence obtained from experiences. The intelligibility of the doctrine of *karma* and its assertions depended upon their internal coherence within the framework of the *karmic* system. And when we examine from this point of view we find out that monistic explanation of the doctrine of *karma* morally seems to be more intelligible and satisfactory doctrine compared to its non-monistic explanation though the experiences do not support it. Because in our experiences we find that in many cases a man suffers not due to any action of his own but due to hostile action of others or due to some other natural events like earthquake and floods etc. Likewise, in many cases it is also seen that a man enjoys not because of any action of his own but because of the other's action. Even if it is admitted that whatever man gets, gets because of his own action, we cannot establish it on the scientific grounds. It always remains a matter of belief and not a matter of fact. The *karma phala* has both a causal and an evaluative components in it and both the components must not be confused. The *karma phala* has a causal component because it causally results from the causal *karmic* process. It has an evaluative component because the *karmic* process from which it results involves in it, judging, evaluating, decision making etc. on the ground of which he merits reward and punishment according to the nature of the done *karmas.* The *karma* produces the *karma phala* not because it is done by this or that desire, being moral or immoral, religious or non-religious etc. but because of its being *karma.* The act force which produces the *karma phala* lies in the nature of *karma* itself. But the *karma* does not guarantee that it will have the same set of consequences/results in all the circumstances which the monistic account of the doctrine of *karma* presupposes. Empirical evidences do not support the *karmic* assumptions mentioned above. But without assuming them, the *karmic* beliefs and assertions cannot be made to be meaningful and intelligible.

Although the monistic and self-centric doctrine of *karma* is a consistent doctrine but those who believe in it do not hold it consistently. They hold different views on the different occasions. Not only this, there are a lot of problems connected with the storage of *karma phala* itself. For example, where and how is the *karma phala* stored to be realised by its doer in subsequent of time ? On this question the *karmavādins* have different opinions Those who do not believe in the existence of God seem to advocate the view that the *karma phala* is stored in the agent's soul or self who performs the *karmas.* But how does it reside in the agent's soul ? In what form does it reside in it? Regarding these questions we do not find any satisfactory answer from them. But those who believe in the existence of God and conceive Him as a moral administrator of the *karmic* world maintain the view that the *karma phala* of *karma* is stored by God and when the right time comes he dispenses it to its doer. But when this question is asked : Why does God do it? Does He do it out of his kindness ? If so, in what form and where does he store the *karma phala* of *karma* of the individuals ? Regarding these questions again we do not find any satisfactory answer from the theistic *karmavādins*. However, both the theistic and the non-theistic *karmavādins* do not hold a consistent theory of the *karmic* beliefs. If the individual's birth is determined by his *karma* as the *karmavādins* advocate, then it must be accepted that one who takes birth had performed certain *karmas* before his birth which is absurd. Because the *karmas* cannot be performed before birth. The performance of *karma* always presupposes the existence of its doer. In other words, the ontological existence of the *kartā* always comes logically prior to his performance of *karma.* If this be so, the *karma phala* of *karma* including the *karma* cannot be said to be the cause of the birth of *kartā*. If the *karma* and its *phala* are the causes of birth, they cannot be said to be the results of birth in respect of the same individual with reference to the same *karmic* process. But since both the theistic and the non-theistic *karmavādins* hold the view that the *karma,* causes and is caused by birth in the same series of the *karmic* process; their accounts of *karma* cannot be said to be self consistent.

Our analysis of the *karmic* assertions shows that even if we assume the identity of *kartā* and *bhoktā* , the conservability and befitting productivity of *karma phala* of *karma*, the *karmic* assertions cannot be made to be sensible without assuming the autonomy of the agent with which the notions of moral responsibility, reward and punishment etc. are associated in the *karmic* world. The notions of responsibility, accountability, deserving, experiencing of rewards and punishments in the forms of pleasure and pain are associated with notion of free action and the notion of free action is essentially linked with the notion of the autonomy of agent. So without assuming of the autonomy of agent, moral responsibility, reward and punishment etc. which the *karmavādins* associate with the *karma phala* of *karma* cannot be made intelligible. The autonomy of agent is not incompatible with the doctrine of *karma.* The autonomy of agent in fact is opposed to fatalism because fatalism denies that the agent has power to change the course of *karmic* events which the doctrine of freedom of the agent presupposes. The doctrine of fatalism maintains that the agent is impotent to do anything by himself. He cannot change the course of *karmic* events by his efforts and power. Whatever he does and exercises is all fated which the doctrine of freedom does not assume. The doctrine of freedom is also opposed to the doctrine of predestination because according to the doctrine of predestination the agent does not have any freedom to choose, to decide, to plan or to do an action in which the freedom or the autonomy of agent consists. The doctrine of predestination asserts that everything that happens in the *karmic* world of the agent is predestinated by God which the doctrine of freedom of the agent denies. The doctrine of *karma* is neither a doctrine of fatalism nor is it a doctrine of predestination because it does not contradict the doctrine of freedom of the agent which the doctrines of fatalism and predestination do. Instead of contradicting the doctrine of freedom, the doctrine of *karma* assumes it. Problems concerning the freedom of agent in connection with the doctrine of *karma* arise when we muddle the doctrine of *karma* with the doctrines of fatalism and predestination or pre-ordination. Though the doctrine of *karma* is not opposed to the law of causality but it is not identical with it. The law of causality asserts that every event has cause. But it does not assert that every event causes another event. Every event may or may not cause another event. While the doctrine of *karma* not only asserts that every action is caused by the agent but also asserts that it causes another event, that is, *karma phala.* The doctrine of *karma* asserts that the *karmas* are caused by a *kartā* and his beliefs, intentions, desires, passions, wills and impressions etc. Not only this, it also asserts that good *karmas* produce good results and bad *karmas* produce bad results and no *karma* produces its reverse result which the doer of *karma* necessarily experiences or realises either in the present life or the life of after death, and that is not asserted by the law of causality. The law of causality does not assert that the doer of *karma* deserves the *karma phala* of *karma* because of his *karma* which the doctrine of *karma* asserts. The doctrine of *karma,* thus, has an ethical component in it which the law of causality lacks. The relation of *karma* and *karma phala* is a causal relation and this relation remains in fact, no matter whether the agent of *karma* himself is affected by the *karma phala* of *karma* or somebody else other than him.

The intelligibility of the doctrine of *karma* and its assertions assume belief in the transmigration of soul and *karmic* residues. But the belief in the transmigration of soul neither entails nor is entailed by the belief in the transmigration of *karmic* residues. Both the beliefs are different though are mutually compatible. But one who believes in the theory of transmigration of soul and *karmic* residues is bound to believe in *saṁsāra* because it is *saṁsāra* in which the transmigration of soul and *karmic* residues are conceived to be possible. But one who believes in *saṁsāra* is not necessarily bound to believe in the identity of a thing belonging to it; because the notion of *saṁsāra* does not essentially involve in its meaning the notion of identity. The transmigration of soul with the *karmic* residues assumes the identity of actor and action in the continuity of the series of life. It is the identity of *kartā-bhoktā -karma phala* that makes theory of rebirth or transmigration meaningful and intelligible. To deny this would amount to mean the denial of responsibility in the senses of accountability and deserving which in the view of *karmavādins* the agent owes and earns on the account of his deeds. Ethical responsibility assumes the continuity of the ethical agent and the continuity of the ethical agent assumes the identity and persistency of agent and *karma phala* of his *karma* in some sense or the other, without assuming of which neither the notion of identity of the agent makes any sense nor the notions of rebirth and *karma phala. Karma, saṁsāra* and transmigration are conceptually and essentially connected. The *karmavādins* those who believe in the transmigration of soul also believe in the transferability of *karmic* residues from one life to another life so far as the life of a particular individual is concerned, that is, agent but deny by and large its transferability from the life of one person to another person. In other words, the *karmavādins* believe that the *karmic* residues pass from one life to another life of a person, but they do not believe that the *karmic* residues pass from one individual's life to another individual's life which can be entitled as genetic *karmas.* Those *karmavādins* who believe in it, their *karmic* accounts suffer from the fallacies of *kṛtapraṇāśa* and *akṛtābhyāgama* and fail to provide a satisfactory explanation for all that happens in the individual's life, good or bad. Why the *karmic* residues pass from one life to another life so far the life of an individual is concerned but do not pass from one individual's life to another individual's life is no doubt a relevant question which the *karmavādins* seem to have not answered. The thesis of non-transferability of the *karmic* residues from one individual's life to another individual's life, if at all possible, can be said to be possible only when we assume the inseparability of the individual's *karmic* residues with his soul or self till their fructification. Not only this, we have to further assume the plurality of the soul. Then and then alone the thesis of the non-transferability of *karma* from one individual's life to another individual's life can be maintained consistently. All the *karmavādins* believe that freedom from the *karmic* bondage is possible with embodied or disembodied body but how it is possible and what makes it possible about these questions they have different opinions. Some classical Indian schools of thought say that freedom from the *karmic* bondage is possible through knowledge and knowledge alone; while the other classical Indian schools of thought say that right knowledge and right action both are essentially required to get freedom from the *karmic* bondage. But still the fact remains that they all believe that freedom from the *karmic* bondage is not possible without right knowledge. Why they believe that no *karmic* liberation is possible without knowledge is that because they believe that ignorance is the prime cause of *karmic* bondage. But how did the original soul or self get associated with ignorance in the beginning before the unity of soul and body which is conceived as pure consciousness in its essence ? Regarding to this question we do not find any satisfactory answer. But one thing is quite obvious from the analysis of the *karmic* beliefs that if it is the *karma* which causes bondage, then liberation from it is possible only by not doing *karma* and not by doing *karma* regardless of how and in what form it is done. Both the theistic and the non-theistic versions of the doctrine of *karma* suffer from some or the other logical problems. The assumptions on which their accounts are based cannot be validated by means of any evidence obtained from empirical experiences. They are of such kind that they are neither provable nor refutable on the scientific grounds. Therefore, it would not be fair to make use of any pro-and-con empirical evidence in support of their acceptability or validity. The intelligibility of the doctrine of *karma* and its assertions depend upon their internal coherence within the framework of a particular *karmic* system. And when we examine from this point of view, we find that monistic explanation of the doctrine of *karma* relatively is more consistent and satisfactory than its non-monistic one though experiences do not seem to support it. Because in experiences we find that in many cases we suffer not because of our deeds but because of the deeds of others. The theistic account of the doctrine of *karma* suffers from all sorts of disadvantages and inconsistencies from which the theological ethics suffers being its one of the species.

Bibliography

Aurobindo, Sri. *The Problem of Rebirth,* Sri Aurobindo Ashram, Pondicherry, 1952.

Aiyar, Sivaswamy, P.S. *Evolution of Hindu Moral Ideals,* Calcutta, 1935.

Atreya, B.L. *The Spirit of Indian Culture,* The International Standard Publications, Benares, 1952.

Augustine, Saint Aurelius. *Divine Providence and the Problem of Evil,* Tr. Robert, P. Russell, Vol. V, New York : Cima Publishing Co. Inc., 1948.

—,*The Free Choice of the Will,* Tr. Robert . P. Russell, LIX. Washington D.C. : The Catholic University of America Press, 1967.

Allen, G.F. *The Buddha's Philosophy,* London, 1959.

Anand, K.K. *Indian Philosophy,* Bharatiya Vidya Prakashan, 1982.

Buhler, G. (Tr.). *Manava Dharmashastra,* S.B.E. XVV, Oxford, 1886.

Bhargava, Dayanand. *The Jaina Ethics,* Delhi : Motilal Banarsidass, 1968.

Barodia. *Outlines of Jainism,* London, 1916.

Chatterjee, S.C. and Datta, D.M. *An Introduction to Indian Philosophy,* Calcutta, University of Calcutta, 4th ed., 1950.

Davies, John. *The Bhagavad Gītā,* Bharatiya Publishing House, 1979.

Dasgupta, S.N. *A History of Indian Philosophy,* Vol. II, Cambridge, 1932.

Gokhale, B.G. *Indian Thought through the Ages,* Asia Publishing House, 1961.

Gandhi, V.R. *The Karma Philosophy,* Bombay, 1913.

Gopalan, S. *Outlines of Jainism,* New Delhi, 1973.

Guseva, N.R. *Jainism,* Bombay, 1971.

Griswald Hervey De Witt. *The Religion of the Rigveda,* London : Oxford University Press, 1923.

Humphreys, C. *Karma and Rebirth,* London, 1944.

Hospers, John. *An Introduction to Philosophical Analysis,* Allied Publishers Private Ltd., First Indian Reprint, 1971.

Herman, Arthur L. *The Problem of Evil and Indian Thought,* Motilal Banarsidass, 1976.

Hogg, A.G. *Karma and Redemption,* The Christian Literature Society, 1909.

Hiriyanna, M. *Outlines of Indian Philosophy,* George Allen and Unwin, 1932.

Hook, Sidney. *Determinism and Freedom in the Age of Modern Science,* Collier Books, New York, 1961.

Jariwalla, J.S. *Gītā : The Science of Living,* Delhi : Motilal Banarsidass, 1984.

Krishna, Daya. *Indian Philosophy,* Oxford University Press, 1991.

Maitra, S.K. *Ethics of the Hindus,* Calcutta : University of Calcutta, 1956.

_____ *The Spirit of Indian Philosophy,* Benares Hindu University, 1947.

McKenzie, J. *Hindu Ethics,* London, 1922.

Muller, F. Max (Ed.) *Rigveda Saṁhitā,* Vols. I–IV, London, 1890.

_____ (Tr.) *Upaniṣads,* S.B.E. (Series) Vol. I, Oxford, 1879.

Motwani, K. *Manu Dharma Shastra,* Madras, 1958.

Paul, Yevtic. *Karma and Reincarnation in Hindu Religion and Philosophy,* London, 1927.

Prasad, Rajendra. *Karma Causation and Retributive Morality,* I.C.P.R., New Delhi, 1989.

Raja, Kunhan C. *Some Fundamental Problems in Indian Philosophy,* Motilal Banarsidass, Delhi, 1960.

Radhakrishnan, S. *The Bhagavadgītā,* London : George Allen and Unwin, 1948.

_____ *Dhammapada,* London, 1950.

_____ *Indian Philosophy,* London : George Allen and Unwin, 1958.

_____ *The Hindu View of Life,* London : George Allen and Unwin, 1927.

_____ *The Principal Upaniṣads,* London : George Allen and Unwin, 1953.

Stevenson, S. *The Heart of Jainism,* London : Oxford, 1915.

Sogani, K.C. *Ethical Doctrine of Jainism,* Sholapur, 1967.

Singh, Balbir. *Foundations of Indian Philosophy,* New Delhi. Orient Longman, 1971.

Sinha, J.N. *Indian Philosophy,* New Central Book Agency, 1987.

Thiroux, Jacques P. *Ethics Theory and Practice,* Collier Macmillan Publishers, London, 1977.

Thakur, U. *Studies in Jainism and Buddhism,* Varanasi, 1964.

Varma, Vishwanath Prasad. *Early Buddhism and Its Origins,* Munshiram Manoharlal, 1973.

Zaehner, R.C. *Hinduism,* Oxford, 1962.

Articles

Balasubrahmanian, R. "The Theory of Karma and the Philosophy of Advaita," *Indian Philosophical Quarterly,* Vol. 6-7, 1979.

Chinchaṛe, Mangala R. "*Kṛtapraṇāśa* and *Akṛtābhyāgama* : An Analysis, Defence and Rationale of the Buddhist Theory of Action, " *Indian Philosophical Quarterly,* Vol. XVIII, 1991.

Datta, Rana. "Transmigration Without a Self", *Darshana International,* Vol. XXXII, 1992.

Ghosh, Dastidar K. "Can there be a Freedom without Responsibility?" *Indian Philosophical Quarterly,* Vol. XI, 1984.

Gangadeen, Ashok. "Comparative Ontology and the Interpretation of 'Karma', *Indian Philosophical Quarterly,* Vol. 6-7, 1979.

Ghosh, Raghunath. "Some Reflections on the Nyāya Theory of Action", *Indian Philosophical Quarterly,* Vol. XVIII, 1991.

Hopkins, W. "Modification of the Karma Doctrine", *Journal of the Royal Asiatic Society,* 1906.

Krishan, Y. "Is Karma Evolutionary?" *Journal of Indian Council of Philosophical Research,* Vol. VI, 1988.

Malkani, G.R. "The Rationale of the Law of Karma", *The Philosophical Quarterly,* January 1965.

Potter, Karl. H. "The Naturalistic Principle of Karma", *Philosophy East and West,* Vol. XIV, 1964.

Sen, Brinda. "The Concept of Kartṛtva in the Nyāya Vaiśeṣika Philosophy", *Indian Philosophical Quarterly,* Vol. XIX, 1992.

Steinkraus, E.W. "Some Criticisms of the Karmic Law", *The Philosophical Quarterly,* October 1965.

Index